*f*P

Also by Steven E. Landsburg

*Fair Play: What Your Child Can Teach You About Economics,
Values, and the Meaning of Life*

The Armchair Economist: Economics & Everyday Life

MORE SEX
IS SAFER SEX

THE UNCONVENTIONAL WISDOM
OF ECONOMICS

Steven E. Landsburg

Free Press
New York   London   Toronto   Sydney

FREE PRESS
A Division of Simon & Schuster, Inc.
1230 Avenue of the Americas
New York, NY 10020

FREE PRESS and colophon are trademarks of Simon & Schuster, Inc.

For information about special discounts for bulk purchases,
please contact Simon & Schuster Special Sales at
1-800-456-6798 or business@simonandschuster.com

Designed by Davina Mock

Manufactured in the United States of America

7   9   10   8   6

Library of Congress Cataloging-in-Publication Data
Landsburg, Steven E.
More sex is safer sex : the unconventional wisdom of economics /
Steven E. Landsburg.
p. cm.
Includes index.
1. Economics—Sociological aspects. 2. Paradoxes. 3. United States—Economic
conditions—21st century. I. Title.

HB849.44 .L36 2007
330—dc22   2006050847
ISBN-13: 978-1-4165-3221-7
ISBN-10:   1-4165-3221-8

To Homeport
in all its manifestations

and

to Lisa
the best surprise of my life

CONTENTS

ACKNOWLEDGMENTS

This is a book about unconventional applications of conventional economics. My first debt is to the many innovative thinkers who devised these applications. Some are named in the chapters and others in the appendix.

I am grateful to the editors of *Slate,* who for ten years have given me remarkable freedom to write about whatever was on my mind. Some of the arguments in this book first appeared in my *Slate* column, though mostly in highly abbreviated form. Here I've taken the opportunity to expand on them considerably.

I am grateful to the thousands of *Slate* readers who have called me to account on points that needed more explanation, and occasionally on points where I was wrong. Several chapters in this book have been greatly improved by what I learned from my readers.

I am grateful to the members of the daily lunch group who have vetted so many of these ideas and contributed to my general education. Most particularly, I owe thanks to Mark Bils, Gordon Dahl, Uta Schönberg, Alan Stockman, and Michael Wolkoff, all of whose comments and criticisms have improved this book.

I am especially grateful to Mark Bils, from whom I've stolen so many ideas and insights that he should probably have been called a coauthor.

I am grateful to my brain trust of brilliant noneconomists who have helped me understand what is and isn't obvious, and have helped me find the perfect words to express some difficult ideas. Thanks especially to Diana Carroll, Michael Raymond Feely, Sharon Fenick, Nathan Mehl, Tim Pierce, John Rosevear, Ellen Keyne Seebacher, and Lisa Talpey. I'm sure that list is not complete.

I am grateful for the encouragement and assistance of Bruce Nichols at Free Press.

And I am grateful to my parents for being proud of me even though they hate the title. For a lot of other things too, come to think of it.

PREFACE:
UNCONVENTIONAL WISDOM

Common sense tells you that promiscuity spreads AIDS, population growth threatens prosperity, and misers make bad neighbors. I wrote this book to assault your common sense.

My weapons are evidence and logic, especially the logic of economics. Logic is most enlightening—and surely most fun—when it challenges us to see the world in a whole new way. This book is about that kind of logic.

Daughters cause divorce. A thirst for revenge is healthier than a thirst for gold. A ban on elephant hunting is bad news for elephants, and disaster assistance is bad news for the people who receive it. Malicious computer hackers should be executed. The most charitable people support the fewest charities. Writing books is socially irresponsible; elbowing your way to the front of the water-fountain line is not. The tall, the slim, and the beautiful earn higher wages—but not for the reasons you think.

Each of those statements is closer to the truth than you might imagine. If your common sense tells you otherwise, remember that common sense also tells you the earth is flat.

What you're about to read is a celebration of all that is counter, original, spare, and strange. I mean every word seriously and every word in fun. These are carefully considered arguments about important issues. But they're also surprising arguments, and surprises are fun. This book will give you new insights about how the world works. Sometimes it might outrage you. I hope it also makes you smile.

PART I

THE COMMUNAL STREAM

Come out to my suburban neighborhood on any crisp October Saturday, and I will show you a minor tragedy: on every lawn a man with a leaf blower, blowing his leaves onto the next man's lawn. Eventually, they all go inside to recover from a hard and thoroughly unproductive morning's work.

That's a bad way to spend a Saturday. If we all ditched our leaf blowers and stayed inside to watch football, we'd all be happier. Unfortunately, human beings are too rational for that. Blowing leaves always makes sense, whatever your neighbors do. If everyone else blows leaves, you'd better blow them also to avoid a double cover. Or, if everyone agrees *not* to blow leaves, your best strategy is to cheat and have the only clean lawn in the neighborhood.

Economics is largely about the surprising and sometimes tragic consequences of rational behavior. When there's an exciting moment at the ballpark, everybody stands up trying to see better, and therefore nobody succeeds. At parties with a lot of simultaneous conversations, everyone speaks loudly to be heard over everyone else, and everyone goes home with a sore throat. Still, it's rational to stand at the ballpark, and to yell at the party. We stand and we yell for the same reason we blow leaves—from exquisite (and entirely rational) concern for our own interests and none for the harm that spills over onto our neighbors.

It's a general principle of economics that *things tend to work out best when people have to live with the consequences of their own behavior,* or, to put it another way, *things tend to work out poorly when the consequences of our actions spill over onto other people.* Simple and obvious as that general principle might sound, it has the power to undermine vast deposits of conventional wisdom. It suggests that the world has too few people, too few misers, and not enough casual sex, but just the right amounts of secondhand smoke and child labor. It implies that a thirst for gold is socially ruinous, but a taste for revenge can be a social godsend. It casts light on why the tall, the thin, and the beautiful earn higher wages. It suggests sweeping reforms of the legal system, the political system, the tax code, and the rule against jumping to the front of the water-fountain line. And it explains why automobile insurance in Philadelphia is so damn expensive.

More mundanely, it tells us there's too much litter on the streets. That's less obvious than you might suppose. Sure, there's a lot of litter, but a lot isn't always the same as too much. After all, some litter *ought* to be there because the alternatives are worse. That half-eaten sandwich you just stepped on? Maybe someone dropped it to avoid being stung by a hornet. The newspaper wrapped around your ankles? Maybe the wind took it while someone chased down the tax returns that had just fallen out of his briefcase. And if you have a heart attack while you're walking down the street with a Popsicle, nobody thinks you should make a beeline for the nearest trash receptacle before collapsing to the ground.

In principle, all the litter on all the sidewalks in all the cities of the world could be there for good reasons. But in fact, I'm sure there *is* too much litter on the streets, and here's how I know: the person who drops a banana peel and the person who slips on it are not usually the same person. That pretty much guarantees that people sometimes drop banana peels even when the cost (to passersby) exceeds the benefit (to the litterbug). Each time that happens, the world becomes a poorer place—and that's what I mean when I say there's too much litter.

"Too much," in other words, is no mere value judgment. It means precisely that in a world with less littering, we could all be happier—just as we could all be happier in a world with fewer leaf blowers and a prohibition on standing at the ballpark.

Whether you're blowing leaves or discarding litter, having children or having sex, saving or spending, smoking or drinking, setting fires or reporting them—your actions have costs and benefits. As long as you *feel* all the costs and benefits, you'll tend to get the quantity right. You'll drop the right number of banana peels, or have the right number of children, or choose the right number of sex partners. But if you feel only the benefits while someone else feels the costs, you'll tend to overindulge. And conversely, if you feel only the costs while someone else feels the benefits, you'll underindulge.

When you're splitting the dinner check, ordering dessert can be a lot like littering—you get the benefits and the costs spill over onto your friends. If the $10 double chocolate mousse is worth only $4 to you, you really shouldn't order it—and you won't, if you're paying your own way. But when you split the check ten ways, that mousse starts to look (to you) like a bargain. You place your order, the group pays $10 to buy you a $4 dessert, and the group (including you) is collectively $6 poorer. That's what I call a bad outcome.

Spillovers cause bad outcomes. That much, I think, is clear, at least in theory. The art is in figuring out what counts as a spillover. Take, for example, the problem of secondhand smoke in restaurants. It's called secondhand smoke precisely because it spills over from one table to another (or from a table into the kitchen). But that doesn't make it a spillover in the relevant sense. It counts as a spillover only if the decision maker ignores it. In this case, there's no spillover because the restaurant owner—the fellow who decides to allow smoking in the first place—is unlikely to ignore something that offends his customers.

Of course, he'll offend some customers no matter what he does. A permissive smoking policy offends nonsmoking customers and employees; a restrictive policy offends the smokers. But it's in the owner's financial interest to keep the offense to a minimum. He bans smoking if the benefits of the ban exceed its costs, and allows it otherwise—for the simple reason that every cost and every benefit hits him directly in the pocketbook, via customers' willingness to spend money in his establishment. He's got all the right incentives so he makes all the right decisions. That's why most economists agree that second-guessing the owner—say, by passing a law that overrides his choices—is a bad idea.

Call it, then, the *communal-stream principle:* Feel free to pollute your own swimming pool, but if your sludge spills over into the stream we all share, you should pay for the damage. Conversely, if you volunteer for cleanup duty, you should get a reward. Otherwise we end up with too much pollution and too few volunteers.

A simple and obvious principle, no? But the consequences can be astonishing.

ONE
MORE SEX IS SAFER SEX

It's true: AIDS is nature's awful retribution for our tolerance of immoderate and socially irresponsible sexual behavior. The epidemic is the price of our permissive attitudes toward monogamy, chastity, and other forms of extreme sexual conservatism.

You've read elsewhere about the sin of promiscuity. Let me tell you about the sin of self-restraint.

Consider Martin, a charming and generally prudent young man with a limited sexual history, who has been gently flirting with his coworker Joan. As last week's office party approached, both Joan and Martin silently and separately entertained the prospect that they just might be going home together. Unfortunately, Fate, through its agents at the Centers for Disease Control, intervened. The morning of the party, Martin happened to notice one of those CDC-sponsored subway ads touting the virtues of abstinence. Chastened, he decided to stay home. In Martin's absence, Joan hooked up with the equally charming

9

but considerably less prudent Maxwell—and Joan got AIDS.

When the cautious Martin withdraws from the mating game, he makes it easier for the reckless Maxwell to prey on the hapless Joan. If those subway ads are more effective against Martin than against Maxwell, they are a threat to Joan's safety. This is especially so when they displace Calvin Klein ads, which might have put Martin in a more socially beneficent mood.

If the Martins of the world would loosen up a little, we could slow the spread of AIDS. Of course, we wouldn't want to push this too far: if Martin loosens up too much, he becomes as dangerous as Maxwell. But when sexual conservatives increase their activity by moderate amounts, they do the rest of us a lot of good. Harvard professor Michael Kremer estimates that the spread of AIDS in England could plausibly be retarded if everyone with fewer than about 2.25 partners per year were to take additional partners more frequently. That would apply to three-fourths of all British heterosexuals between the ages of 18 and 45.

A cautious guy like Martin does the world a favor every time he hits the bars. In fact, he does the world *two* favors. First he improves the odds for everyone who's out there seeking a safe match. The second favor is more macabre, but probably also more significant: If Martin picks up a new partner tonight, he just might pick up an infection as well. That's great. Because then Martin goes home, wastes away in solitude, and eventually dies—taking the virus with him.

If someone has to get infected tonight, I want it to be Martin rather than Promiscuous Pete, who would probably infect another twenty people before finally dying.

I'm always glad to see guys like Martin in the bars. When he takes home an *uninfected* partner, he diverts that partner from a potentially more dangerous liaison. When he takes home an *infected* partner, he diverts that partner from giving the virus to someone who might spread it far and wide. Either way, I sure hope he gets lucky tonight.

Sadly, none of this makes for a good pickup line. You're unlikely to get very far with an approach like "You should sleep with me so you can get infected, die, and take the virus with you." That would be like saying "You should sell your leaf blower so your neighbors' lawns stay cleaner" or "You should stay seated at the ballpark so everyone else can see." The whole point is that what's good for the group can be bad for the individual, and that's why we get bad outcomes.

If multiple partnerships save lives, then monogamy can be deadly. Imagine a country where almost all women are monogamous, while all men demand two female partners per year. Under those circumstances, a few prostitutes end up servicing all the men. Before long, the prostitutes are infected; they pass the disease on to the men; the men bring it home to their monogamous wives. But if each of those monogamous wives were willing to take on one extramarital partner, the market for prostitution would die out, and the virus, unable to spread fast enough to maintain itself, might well die out along with it.

The parable of the monogamous wives has a more profound moral than the legend of Martin and Joan, because it shows that even on a society-wide level, increased promiscuity could retard the epidemic—at least in principle. But what about practice? That's where Professor Kremer's research comes in. With plausibly realistic assumptions about how people choose partners, his work shows that the moral remains essentially the same. When your relatively demure neighbor experiences a rare moment of rakishness, he really is doing his part to combat the deadly scourge.

That's one reason why you should root for Martin to have sex with Joan. Here's another: they'll probably enjoy it.

Enjoyment should never be lightly dismissed. After all, reducing the rate of HIV infection is not the only goal worth pursuing; if it were, we'd outlaw sex entirely. What we really want is to minimize the number of infections resulting from any given number of sexual encounters. That's the same as maximizing the number of (consensual) sexual encounters leading up to any given number of infections. Even if Martin fails to deny Maxwell a conquest, he can at least make someone happy.

If you are a monomaniac whose goal is to minimize the prevalence of AIDS, then you should encourage Martin to have more sex.* But if you are a sensible person whose goal is to maximize the difference between the benefits of sex and the costs of AIDS—then you should encourage Martin to have even *more* sex.

To an economist, it's crystal clear why people with limited sexual pasts choose to supply too little sex in the present: their

---

* Actually, if you are a monomaniac who wants to minimize the prevalence of AIDS and can control *everyone's* behavior, then, as I said earlier, you should outlaw sex entirely. But if you are a monomaniac who wants to minimize the prevalence of AIDS and can control only Martin's behavior while taking Maxwell's as given, then you should encourage Martin to have more sex, not less.

services are underpriced. If sexual conservatives could effectively advertise their histories, HIV-conscious suitors would compete to lavish them with attention. But that doesn't happen, because conservatives are hard to identify. Insufficiently rewarded for relaxing their standards, they relax their standards insufficiently.

When you take a new sex partner, you bear some costs and you reap some benefits. Those are your business. You also impose costs and benefits on others, and those are everyone else's business. If you have a history of reckless promiscuity, that's a cost. Everyone's fishing for partners in a great communal stream and you've polluted that stream just by entering it.

But if you've always been cautious and selective, you're likely to *raise* the average quality of the partner pool. Just by jumping into the stream, you make it purer. Thanks to you, everyone who goes fishing for a partner tonight has a better chance of catching a safe one.

Like any other communal stream, the stream of partners has too many polluters and too few volunteers to clean it up. The reason factory owners don't do enough to protect the environment is that they're insufficiently rewarded for environmental protection (or insufficiently punished for neglecting it). They reap *some* rewards (even factory owners like clean water and clean air), but most of the benefits go to total strangers. Likewise, the reason Martin might not do enough to fight the scourge of AIDS (by sleeping with Joan) is that, while he certainly would reap *some* rewards (such as sexual pleasure), many of the benefits would go to Joan's future partners, and their future partners.

The flip side of the analogy is that Martin's chastity is a form of pollution—chastity pollutes the sexual environment by reducing the fraction of relatively safe partners in the dating pool. Factory owners pollute too much because they have to breathe only a fraction of their own pollution; Martin stays home alone too much because he bears only a fraction of the consequences.

The pollution analogy is so powerful that it dictates the moral of virtually any story you could tell. To conclude that Martin's coupling with Joan *slows the epidemic,* you have to make some assumptions about what Joan and Maxwell and all of *their* potential partners would be doing if Martin stayed home. But to conclude that Martin's coupling with Joan *makes the world a better place* (where "better" accounts for both the costs of disease and the benefits of sex), you don't need any of those assumptions. It is a quite general principle that when goods (such as Martin's sexual services) are underpriced, they are undersupplied.

Here, then, is what we know:

When sexual conservatives relax their standards, benefits spill over onto their neighbors. That alone is enough to tell us that the world would be a better place if we could loosen these people up a little.

There is, however, more than one way for the world to become a better place. Maybe the epidemic slows down. Maybe people enjoy more sex. Maybe the epidemic speeds up, but people enjoy so *much* more sex that it's worth it.

Pure theory—in the guise of the communal-stream principle—tells us that at least one of those good things must happen. Professor Kremer's research suggests that *both* good things happen: we get more sex *and* less illness.

If all you want to do is slow down the epidemic, Professor Kremer's research says that more sex is a good thing. But if you want to maximize the excess of benefits over costs, then even *more* sex is an even *better* thing.

* * *

So: how do we encourage Martin (and others like him) to have more sex?

I wish this book could nudge him in the right direction, but sadly, there's no reason why it should—even if he reads and understands it completely. (Don't let that stop you from buying him a copy, though.) Martin has already chosen the activity level that's right for him. He's not likely to adjust that level just because he learns that a bunch of strangers—namely, Joan's future partners and *their* future partners—would appreciate it.

Martin, being human, tends to concentrate on what's good for Martin, not what's good for the society he lives in. You can make a polluting factory owner understand that he's hurting his neighbors, but that's not the same as convincing him to stop.

So we need something more effective than mere education. Extrapolating from their usual response to environmental issues, I assume that liberals would attack the problem of excessive sexual temperance through coercive legislation. But as a devotee of the price system, I'd prefer to encourage good behavior through a well-designed system of subsidies.

In other words, we could pay people to have more sex with more partners. But that's not ideal, because we don't want *everyone* to have more sex with more partners. Maxwell, for example, is quite oversexed enough as it is. The problem is to subsidize Martin's sexual awakening without simultaneously subsidizing Maxwell's genuine excess.

So we should pay people for having sex only if they are relatively inexperienced. Unfortunately, that doesn't work very well either—not as long as Maxwell can lie about his past and keep a straight face long enough to collect his handout.

What we need is a reward that Martin values and Maxwell doesn't—like, say, a library card. I'm guessing that Maxwell, with his busy social life, doesn't spend a lot of time at the library.

That's a definite improvement, but it's still imperfect. When Martin arrives at the circulation desk looking appropriately smug and disheveled, how can the librarian know whether he's really fulfilled his coital obligations or is just putting on a good show?

Let's try again: We need a reward that's of no value to Martin unless he actually has sex. And as before, it should be something the cautious Martin values more than the promiscuous Maxwell does.

I can think of only one reward that fits both criteria: free (or heavily subsidized) condoms. To reap the benefits of a free condom, Martin has to have sex. And Martin probably values a free condom considerably more than Maxwell does. Here's why: Martin's almost surely not infected yet, so a condom has a good chance to save his life. Maxwell, by contrast, knows he might have the virus already, so a condom at this point is less likely to make a difference. Subsidized condoms could be just the ticket for luring Martin out of his shell without stirring Maxwell to a new frenzy of activity.

As it happens, there is another reason to subsidize condoms. Condom use itself is underrewarded. When you use a condom, you protect both yourself and your future partners (and your future partners' future partners), but you are rewarded (with a lower chance of infection) only for protecting yourself. Your future partners can't observe your past condom use and therefore can't reward it with extravagant courtship. That means you fail to capture all the benefits you're conferring. As a result, condoms are underused.

In other words, people use too few condoms for the same reason they have too little sex. When Martin has sex with Joan, that's good for Joan's future partners. When Martin uses a condom, that's good for *Martin's* future partners. In neither case do the future partners get a fair opportunity to influence Martin's behavior.

It's frequently argued that subsidized (or free) condoms have an upside and a downside. The upside is that they reduce the risk from a given encounter, and the alleged downside is that they encourage more encounters. But that's not an upside and a downside—it's two upsides. Without the subsidies, people don't use enough condoms, and without the subsidies, the sort of people who most value condoms don't have enough sex partners.

The main drawback to subsidizing condoms is that they're not very expensive to begin with. You can reduce the price of a condom from a dollar all the way down to zero without having much impact on people's sexual choices.

Our goal, then, should be to drive the price of condoms *below* zero, by rewarding people who use them. In other words, we should pay a bounty for used condoms. The best of all possible bounties would be one that is more valuable to abstemious Martins than to promiscuous Maxwells. With that in mind, the journalist Oliver Morton has made the marvelous suggestion that if at least some abstemiousness is due to shyness and the inability to find partners (while the promiscuous have relatively little trouble in this regard), then the answer might be to establish a government-funded dating service: bring us a used condom and we'll get you a date.*

---

* When I expressed concern about the ease of fakery in this context, Mr. Morton responded: "Yes, I worried about the faking problem. But anyone who's willing to go to that kind of trouble should probably be encouraged on the dating market anyway."

The entire problem—along with the entire case for subsidies—would vanish if our sexual pasts could somehow be made visible, so that future partners could reward past prudence and thereby provide appropriate incentives. Perhaps technology can ultimately make that solution feasible. (I imagine the pornography of the future: "Her skirt slid to the floor and his gaze came to rest on her thigh, where the imbedded monitor read 'This site has been accessed 314 times.'")

Or, as one of my *Slate* readers suggested, we could have an online service to record negative HIV test results. You'd type in your prospective partner's name and get a response like "Last negative test result 7/4/2006." Or, to protect privacy, you'd type in not a name but an ID number provided by the partner. Your screen could show both a test result and a photo to avoid fake IDs. This strikes me as such a good idea that I can't figure out why nobody's doing it yet. Until then, the best we can probably do is to make condoms inexpensive—and get ride of those subway ads.

Addendum

In 1996, *Slate* magazine published an abbreviated version of this chapter that generated hundreds of email responses. Quite a few of those responses were both thoughtful and interesting, and helped me to improve the presentation you've just read. Others contained nothing but a line or two of invective. To those, I usually responded with a short note that read "I'm sorry, but from the email you sent me I was not able to ascertain at exactly which point you stopped following the argument. If you can be more precise about where you got lost, I'll do my best to make it clearer." In a remarkable number of cases, I got responses that were both thoughtful and apologetic, and a few of those led to multiround correspondences that taught me something.

Other readers seemed bound and determined to miss the point by miles. One, brandishing his credentials as a medical doctor, termed the column "particularly unfortunate" and—in a letter that was published in a subsequent issue of *Slate*—explained why:

> We are at a stage in the HIV epidemic in which heterosexual spread is becoming increasingly significant. Casual readers . . . may justify increasing their sexual-risk-taking behavior. Unfortunately, failure, lasting in a shortened lifetime, can result from a sexually successful one-night stand.
>
> For an appropriate sequel, the editor of *Slate* might solicit an article . . . defending Russian roulette as statistically OK but cautioning that three loaded chambers is too risky.

One of the great discoveries of nineteenth-century economics was the principle of *comparative advantage,* according to which people are most successful when they stick to the things they're good at. (It's actually quite a bit subtler than that, but this oversimplified version suffices for the application I'm about to make.) The principle of comparative advantage explains why some people become medical doctors, while other, different, people go into fields (such as economics) that require at least a minimal ability to reason logically.

There is nothing—not one word—in the chapter you've just read or in the original *Slate* article that could provoke any reader to increased sexual-risk-taking behavior. Indeed, the whole point is that the relatively chaste have too little sex because it is *not* in their interest to behave otherwise. If you and your spouse are monogamous, you likely won't get any sexually transmitted diseases. If I point out that your continued monogamy is potentially deadly to your neighbors, I don't expect you'll rush to risk your life for theirs.

Imagine this scenario: I write an article explaining that when firms put filters on their smokestacks, they perform a positive social service. Unfortunately, installing filters cuts into firms' profits, so they install fewer filters than the rest of us prefer. Therefore we might want to consider subsidizing such installations.

Along comes our medical doctor to argue that: (a) filters reduce profits and are therefore a bad thing, (b) my article is "particularly unfortunate" because "casual readers who own factories may increase their anti-pollution efforts," and (c) if we're going to argue for anti-pollution equipment, we might as well solicit an article advising firms to convert all their assets into rowboats and then sink them.

Points (a) and (b) are both flat wrong (though if casual readers *were* so foolish—or so uncommonly altruistic—as to increase their anti-pollution efforts on the basis of an article that provides no justification for doing so, we could all be grateful for their foolishness, and would consider the article the very opposite of "particularly unfortunate").* Point (c) is a non sequitur perfectly analogous to the good doctor's comments about Russian roulette; such a strategy confers no benefits on the neighbors and thus is completely off-topic.

I've given this much space to my physician-correspondent because his comments were echoed by several others, who ex-

---

* To be entirely explicit about the analogy: Installing filters is like becoming more promiscuous; it hurts you and helps your neighbors. The fact that something hurts you does not make it a bad thing, and the fact that it helps your neighbors does not make you want to go out and do it. On the other hand, if a few of my readers (medical students, perhaps?) are so easily confused that they go out and have more sex because of these arguments, that's probably something the rest of us can be thankful for.

pressed concern that naive readers would misunderstand the argument so completely that they'd all become highly promiscuous Maxwells and ultimately extinguish the human species. A few even urged me to publish a retraction for precisely that reason. In other words, they argued that ideas should be suppressed because somebody might misunderstand them. That's a position with a long and sordid history of which I'd rather not become a part.

Here are some more questions that came up often enough to make it worth recording the answers:

> *Question 1:* You say that a bit more promiscuity would lead to less AIDS. If that were true, would it not follow that an enormous increase in promiscuity could defeat the disease altogether? And is that conclusion not manifestly absurd?
>
> *Answer:* The "conclusion" is indeed manifestly absurd, but it is not a legitimate conclusion. Large changes and small changes don't always have similar consequences. I believe that if I ate a bit less, I would live a bit longer. But I do not believe that if I stopped eating entirely, I would live forever.

> *Question 2:* In the words of one reader, "a spoonful of promiscuity will only *slow* the disease; self-restraint can *stop* it." In view of that, is it not irresponsible to tout the merits of promiscuity without also emphasizing the merits of self-restraint?
>
> *Answer:* This is like arguing that traffic lights can

only *reduce* the number of auto accidents, while banning cars can *stop* auto accidents; therefore, it would be irresponsible to tout the merits of traffic lights.

The problem with such reasoning is that banning cars, like banning sex outside of long-term relationships, is neither realistic nor clearly desirable—it's not going to happen, and if it did happen, we'd probably be less happy, despite the attendant decrease in mortality.

In any event, everybody already knows that a perfectly monogamous society would not have an AIDS problem. I prefer to write about things that are both true and *surprising*. As a writer, I dare to hope that there are readers who are actually interested in learning something.

Question 3: Okay, there are benefits to increased promiscuity. But there can also be benefits to increased chastity. Isn't it inconsistent to subsidize one without subsidizing the other?

Answer: No, because there is a critical difference between the two kinds of benefit. The benefits of your promiscuity go to others; the benefits of your chastity go to you. Thus you already have sufficient incentives on the pro-chastity side.

Question 4: Didn't you leave out some things that might be important?

Answer: Absolutely. For one thing, a change in human behavior could trigger a burst of evolution on the part of the virus. I doubt that consideration is important in this context (though it's surely important in others), but maybe I'm wrong. For another, at least one reader contended that slight increases in promiscuity are impossible because they trigger cultural changes that lead to *large* increases in promiscuity. I doubt that he's right, but I can't prove he's wrong.

TWO

BE FRUITFUL AND MULTIPLY

Ted Baxter, the anchorman on the old *Mary Tyler Moore Show,* planned to have six children in hopes that one of them would grow up to solve the world's population problem. Ted was a poor newscaster but a natural economist. His basic insight was impeccable: people solve problems, and when there are more people, more problems get solved.*

The reason you are wealthier than your grandparents, and the reason your grandchildren will be wealthier than you, is that each generation free-rides on the inventiveness of its ancestors. A generation ago, your parents were free to choose among three television channels, probably broadcasting in black and white, showing programs that could not be taped for later viewing. They used electric typewriters, of which the latest models featured a marvelous innovation: a "delete" key that enabled you

---

* Portions of this chapter are excerpted from my earlier book *Fair Play.*

automatically to erase the last character you had typed. If you wanted to erase the character before that one you were out of luck.

For many of the comforts we enjoy today, we can be grateful to the inventors of cable television, video recorders, and the personal computer—and to the stroke of good fortune that prevented their parents from joining Zero Population Growth.

The engine of prosperity is technological progress, and the engine of technological progress is people. Ideas come from people. The more people, the more ideas. The more ideas, the more we prosper.

Michael Kremer, the Harvard economist, has gathered data from a million years of human history and prehistory to support the theory that population growth drives technological progress, technological progress drives economic growth, and—to complete the virtuous circle—economic growth drives population growth, because wealthier communities can support more children. Professor Kremer's research leads him to quote Ted Baxter with approval.

Professor Kremer bases his argument on the presumption that a world with twice as many people will have twice as many natural-born geniuses. Thus a bigger population develops better technology for the same reason that the biggest high schools usually have the best football teams. But it's even better than that. A great quarterback is a great quarterback, but a great inventor can teach *everyone* to be more productive. And the quarterback's contribution ends when he graduates, but the inventor's contribution lives on forever.

There are two reasons why the gains from population size could exceed even the optimistic estimates of Professor Kremer. First, geniuses tend to inspire each other, so that 2,000 geniuses might generate *more* than twice as many ideas as

1,000 could.* Second, a larger population means a larger market for inventions, and hence an incentive for inventors to work harder. So population growth not only adds to the number of natural-born geniuses—it also encourages those of us with more ordinary talents to stretch those talents to their limits.

In fact, two economists at the Federal Reserve Bank of Richmond, in research recently published by the *American Economic Review*, argue that the Industrial Revolution—and the massive ongoing growth spurt that it triggered—had to wait until world markets grew big enough to reward large-scale innovation by entrepreneurs.

Modern humans first appeared about one hundred thousand years ago. For the next 99,800 years or so, pretty much everyone lived just above the subsistence level—on the modern U.S. equivalent of $400 to $600 a year. In a few fortunate times and places, it was a bit more than that, but almost never more than about twice as much. There were usually tiny nobilities who lived far better indeed, but numerically those nobilities were quite insignificant. If you'd been born any time before the late eighteenth century, it's astronomically probable that you'd have lived on the equivalent of under $1000 a year—just like your parents and your grandparents, and just like your children and your grandchildren.

Then, in the late eighteenth century—just a couple of hundred years ago, maybe ten generations—something happened. People started getting richer. And richer and richer still. Per capita income, at least in the West, began to grow at the unprece-

---

* On the other hand, one could argue that geniuses also tend to intimidate each other: why spend your youth working to develop cold fusion if the genius next door is likely to beat you to it and get the patent?

dented rate of about three-quarters of a percent per year. A couple of decades later, the same thing was happening around the world. After thousands of years of stagnation, life started improving from one year to the next, and before long people started taking improvements for granted. Today we expect our cars, our computers, our medicines, and our entertainment systems to keep dazzling us with something new. But that's not how it was before the Industrial Revolution. That three-quarters of a percent annual growth rate, once it got under way, must have seemed miraculous.

But then it got better. By the twentieth century, per capita real incomes—that is, incomes adjusted for inflation—were growing by 1.5 percent per year, on average, and since 1960—for almost fifty years now—they've been growing by about 2.3 percent. Let me give you an idea of what those growth rates mean to the average American.

If you're a middle-class American earning $50,000 a year, and you expect your children, twenty-five years from now, to occupy that same modest rung on the economic ladder, then with a 2.3 percent growth rate, they'll be earning the inflation-adjusted equivalent of $89,000 per year. *Their* children, another twenty-five years down the line, will earn $158,000 a year. And if that 2.3 percent growth rate continues, then in fewer than four hundred years, your descendants will earn about $1 million *per day*—a little less than Bill Gates's current income, but at least in the ballpark. I want to make clear that these are not some future inflation-ravaged dollars we're talking about; they're the equivalent of a million of *today's* dollars.

If it strikes you as implausible that we could ever generate that kind of wealth, keep in mind that this is a conservative extrapolation of a centuries-old trend. It assumes today's 2.3 percent growth rate will continue unchanged, whereas in fact, growth has been accelerating since it first got underway two hundred years ago. Keep in mind too that every historical advance has seemed wildly implausible until it happened. In the first century AD, Sextus Julius Frontinus wrote that "inventions reached their limit long ago, and I see no hope for further development."

Against a backdrop like that, the temporary ups and downs of the business cycle seem like a fantastically minor phenomenon. In the 1930s, we had a Great Depression, when income levels fell back to where they'd been about twenty years earlier. For a few years, people had to live the way their parents had *always* lived—and they considered it almost intolerable. The underlying expectation—that the present is supposed to be better than the past—is a new phenomenon in history. No eighteenth-century politician would have dreamed of asking "Are you better off than you were four years ago?" because it never would have occurred to anyone that they *ought* to be better off than they were four years ago.

Rising income is only part of the story. Not only are we richer than ever before, we also work less and have better-quality products. One hundred years ago, the average American workweek was over sixty hours; today it's under thirty-five. One hundred years ago, only 6 percent of manufacturing workers took vacations; today it's 90 percent. One hundred years ago, men entered the full-time labor force in their early teens; today labor-force participation by young teenagers is essentially zero. One hundred years ago, only 26 percent of male workers retired by age 65; today over 80 percent of 65-year-old males have retired. One hundred years ago, the average housekeeper spent twelve hours a day on laundry, cooking, cleaning, and sewing; today it's about three hours.

Here's a typical laundry day for a housewife in 1900: First, she ports water to the stove, and heats it by burning wood or coal. Then she cleans the clothes by hand, rinses them, wrings them out (either by hand or with a mechanical wringer), then hangs them to dry and moves on to the oppressive task of ironing, using heavy flatirons that are heated continuously on the stove. The whole process takes about eight-and-a half-hours and she walks over a mile in the process. We know this because the United States government used to hire researchers to follow housewives around and record every step they took.

It wasn't just laundry: At the beginning of the twentieth century, most households had no running water and few had central heating. So routine housework included lugging seven tons of coal and 9,000 gallons of water around the house every year.

By 1945, our heroine probably had a washing machine. Now her laundry chores took just two-and-a-half hours instead of eight-and-a-half and instead of walking a mile, she walked just 665 feet. Today, so that you don't have to waste a single moment keeping an eye on your laundry, you can get a washing machine that emails you when it's done.

Today in the United States of America among the very poorest of the poor—those with household incomes under $15,000 a year—99 percent have refrigerators (83 percent of them frost-free); 64 percent have air-conditioning; 97 percent have color TVs and over two-thirds have cable; 60 percent have washers and dryers. Almost half have personal computers, and most of those have Internet access.

As far as the quality of the goods we buy, try picking up an electronics catalogue from oh, say, 2001 and ask yourself whether there's anything there you'd consider owning. That was the year my friend Ben spent $600 for a 1.3-megapixel digital camera. It weighed a pound and a half and wrote to a *floppy disk!* Go ahead and pick up that catalogue, and I guarantee you'll be astonished by how much better products have gotten in just the past few years.

Or, if you prefer, take a product like health care. Would you rather purchase today's health care at today's prices, or the health care of say, 1970 at 1970 prices? I don't know any informed person who would choose 1970, which means that despite all the hype, health care now is a better bargain than it's ever been. Our lives are better and our lives are longer. The probability that a 20-year-old has a living grandmother today is higher than the probability that a 20-year-old had a living mother a hundred years ago.

The moral is that increases in measured income—even the phenomenal increases of the past two centuries—don't accurately reflect improvements in our economic condition. The average middle-class American might have a smaller measured income than the European monarchs of the Middle Ages, but that does not prevent the American from leading a more luxurious life. I suspect that Henry VIII would have traded half his kingdom for modern plumbing, a lifetime supply of penicillin, and access to the Internet.

Will these trends continue? Of course, nobody knows—just as nobody knows whether the earth will be destroyed by an asteroid in ten years. But we can make educated guesses about probabilities. What we do know is that economic growth, despite some minor ups and downs, has continued—and accelerated—pretty much unabated for the past two hundred years. We also know that all that growth was fueled by technological progress. And we can reasonably conjecture that the reason we're not running out of fuel is that technological progress replenishes itself: each new idea makes the next new idea easier to come by. Add to that Professor Kremer's argument that increasing wealth allows us to support a larger population, which in turn figures out new ways to create wealth, and there is excellent reason for optimism.

A skeptic could easily point to countries where large populations coexist with abysmal economic conditions.* But without exception, those are countries where the natural advantages of population size—a larger pool of geniuses and an abundance of trading partners—are undercut by government policies that limit both the rewards for ingenuity and the opportunities for trade. When the advantages of population growth are eliminated, only the disadvantages remain.†

And that's not all. A large population brings many blessings besides prosperity. We value our neighbors not just as potential trading partners, but as potential friends and potential mates. We value our children for reasons that have little to do with their earning capacity. A lot of people prefer New York to Montana, or Calcutta to the surrounding countryside, because there are advantages to living in a crowd.

A world with more people is a world with more diversity. Chamber music, parasailing, and Ethiopian restaurants can survive only where the population is large enough to support them. In a less populated world, there wouldn't have been enough readers to justify publishing this book. (No wisecracks, please.)

People who live in Manhattan or Detroit might complain about the crowds, but as long as they remain in Manhattan or Detroit it's hard to take them seriously. There are plenty of sparsely populated areas in the United States, and anybody who wants to move there is free to do so. Manhattanites will tell you

---

* A counterskeptic could easily point to Hong Kong.

† One could also argue that the populations of individual countries are not the relevant variables. Because anything that's invented in one place can easily be copied in other places, it could be only the *world* population that's important.

that they stay in New York because of the theater or the symphony or the job opportunities—but that's just another way of saying they stay in New York because it's crowded.

Those are some big benefits of population growth. Most importantly, they're *spillover* benefits: when *I* decided to have a child, *you* were a winner. To decide whether the earth is over- or underpopulated, we'll want to weigh those spillover benefits against any spillover costs we can think of.

But first let's acknowledge the benefits and costs that *don't* spill over. The day my daughter was born, my family's per capita income fell by one-third (because it was now shared among three people instead of two). Without offsetting benefits, that would have been one of the worst days of my life. Instead, it was the best. (Indeed, the economist Peter Bauer once observed that if per capita income were the only measure of human happiness, then the birth of a farm animal would be a blessing and the birth of a child would be a curse.)

Large as they are, those private (nonspillover) costs and benefits are quite irrelevant to the population issue, because people already have every incentive to account for them when they calibrate their family sizes. And they do. Family sizes are quite sensitive to changes in economic conditions. All over the world, whenever the economic rewards for education have risen, family sizes have shrunk so parents can afford to educate their children. (This accounts for the fact that family sizes of seven, eight, or nine children were common in the nineteenth century but rare today.) And all over the world, decreases in child mortality are associated with decreases in fertility—in other words, if more of your children survive, you'll compensate by having fewer children. This too suggests that most children are the products of choice, not chance.

On a smaller scale, the Austrian government has recently been kind enough to run a genuine controlled experiment. First-time mothers in Austria are entitled to a year of parental leave, during which they receive monthly checks from the government. In 1990, the law was liberalized to allow many mothers a second year of leave—provided their second child was born within two years of the first.

The change was abrupt. If your first child was born in June 1990, you played by the old rules; if your first child was born in July, you played by the new ones. And you didn't get to choose which rules you played by: the changes weren't even proposed until November 1989, when it was too late for people to plan their conceptions accordingly.

The result: compared to June first-time mothers, July first-time mothers were 15 percent more likely to have a second child within two years. And ten years down the line, the July mothers still had larger families.

In other words, parents respond to incentives, even relatively small incentives (the Austrian government checks were for the equivalent of about $350 a month). That means they make pretty sensitive cost-benefit calculations, whether or not they do it consciously.

From the fact that I wanted a child, you can infer that I thought she was worth the expense—whatever costs I felt, the benefits were greater. Presumably your parents felt the same way about you; otherwise you wouldn't be here. On top of that, there were spillover benefits—you (like my daughter) contribute to the world's stock of ideas, diversity, and love. But it still doesn't follow that the world should applaud either my fertility or your parents'. Offsetting those spillover benefits, we still have spillover costs to account for.

But beware. It's easy to get confused about what spills over and what doesn't. Take resource consumption, for example. As you go through life, you claim a share of the world's food, petroleum, land, and other resources. You might think that by claiming those resources, you slightly impoverish each of your neighbors. But that's not right. To see why not, think about *how* you claim those resources. Some you produce (say by growing an apple); surely that doesn't impoverish anyone. Some you trade for; that doesn't impoverish anyone either. (You might take an apple or a gallon of oil from me, but I get something I value even more in return.) Most of the remainder you inherit, and only then do you diminish someone else's share. But your inheritance does not take resources from humanity in general; it takes them from your siblings in particular.

That's a critical point and it's often missed. When people think about overpopulation, they typically imagine that if, for example, I had not been born, everyone else would have a slightly bigger share of the pie. Actually, if I had not been born, both of my sisters would have a much bigger share of the pie and everybody else's share would be pretty much the same as it is now.

This simple observation suggests that each family can choose its own population growth rate, and for the most part, no family has to be impoverished by population growth unless it wants to be. If you and I each own a thousand acres, and my family doubles its size every generation while yours practices zero population growth, then in ten generations my descendants will own less than an acre apiece, while your descendants each still own a thousand acres. The costs of my family's hyperfertility are no concern of yours.

There are certainly exceptions. If my family gets too large, we might decide to make war on your family; that's a spillover cost you could have some legitimate concerns about. If I become a thief, a major polluter, or a ward of the government, you might legitimately wish I'd never been born. But fortunately, most people acquire only a small fraction of their resources through conquest, theft, or government largesse. So, unless you are very atypical, most of your resource consumption is not a spillover cost.

Some families prefer to have *wealthy* descendants; others prefer to have *lots* of descendants. But as long as our choices don't impinge on each other, that's not a policy issue; it's an opportunity to celebrate diversity.

Thomas Malthus, that most dismal of scientists, welcomed the nineteenth century with a gloomy prophecy of uncontrolled population growth leading inexorably to mass starvation and human misery. What went wrong with that prediction? It turns out that Malthus made not one great mistake, but two: he miscalculated the benefits of population growth and he miscalculated the costs.

On the benefit side, Malthus failed to foresee that technological progress—fueled by the very population growth that he found so alarming—would enable food production to grow (and continue growing) at better than geometric rates. And on the cost side, he failed to realize that each family is free to choose its own population growth rate, so that no matter what's happening to the food supply, no family has to be impoverished by population growth unless it wants to be.

* * *

You might think of *overcrowding* as a spillover cost of population growth, but in fact overcrowding is not a cost at all, because it's one hundred percent voluntary. You don't have to live in a crowded place unless you want to. You can enjoy the cultural benefits of a population center like New York or you can enjoy the tranquillity and space of rural Virginia. Eliminate the crowding in New York and all you've done is eliminate one of the choices.

Chicagoans are free to move to Nebraska and Calcuttans are free to move to the countryside. The reason they don't is that for all their complaining, they prefer the crowds. For goodness' sake, why are rents so high in Manhattan if not because people place a high value on living near others?

Not that New Yorkers will admit it. In one recent survey, 37 percent of New Yorkers said they'd leave the city if they could. Of course, since none of them had left the city, and since all of them could, the only proper conclusion is that 37 percent of New Yorkers lie to pollsters.

Crowds are not a problem because if you don't like the crowds you can leave. I know it seems like there are a lot of people in the world, but I'm not the first to observe that they all fit in the Grand Canyon if you stack them right. Or, if you don't like that image, try this one, which I got from the economist Thomas Sowell: take the state of Texas, divide it into lots of 5,000 square feet, put a house on each lot, and put a family of four in each house. You've just housed the entire world population.

Many other apparent spillovers are also illusory. You might think, for example, that you impose costs on me when you bid up the price of cars or apply for a job I was hoping to get. But those are not true costs, because they come packaged with offsetting benefits. When the price of cars goes up, sellers gain as much as buyers lose. If you prove a stronger job candidate than I am, my loss is the employer's (and his customers') gain.

* * *

Professional alarmists ask all the wrong questions. First: how many people can the earth support? That's entirely the wrong question, because the earth is not a decision maker. There's no need for you to worry how many people the earth can support; you are free to concentrate on how many people *your share* of the earth can support and calibrate your family size accordingly. If somebody else decides to stretch his share a little thinner, only a busybody would protest.

Or: what will we do when the oil (or some other exhaustible resource) runs out? That's another wrong question, because it implicitly assumes our oil consumption imposes costs on our neighbors rather than ourselves. The question would vanish in a world without neighbors. Robinson Crusoe will never overuse his oil. He might wish he had more of it, but given the amount he's got, he has every incentive to make the best possible decisions about how much to use now and how much to save for the future.

The same is true if Robinson has children and grandchildren he cares about. Every gallon he burns is a gallon taken from his grandchildren, and he fully accounts for that when he makes his choice.

Ah, but what if there are many families on the island, and Robinson cares only about his own? There's still no problem, and for the same reason as before: Robinson's family owns either some oil or some other assets that they expect to trade for oil, and makes its own decisions about conservation. Other families make other decisions. There is still no need for those decisions to impinge on each other.

If you're worried about not having enough oil for your family, you can pare down your family size accordingly. If you think others are recklessly ignoring the impending catastrophe, that's not a cause for concern; it's a business opportunity—buy an oil well and your children will be rich! And if those other families are truly reckless, it costs you nothing to let them make their own mistakes.

Here's the *right* question: was your birth—or any child's birth—a blessing or a curse?

It's hopeless to settle this question by listing all the costs and benefits of sharing the world with other people, because you never know what you've overlooked. After an evening stuck in summer traffic, you'll remember that the driver in front of you imposed a cost, but you'll forget that the guy who invented car air-conditioning conferred a benefit. You'll remember the shopper who fumbled with coupons and slowed down the checkout line, but you'll forget the kind stranger who helped you change a tire on a cold winter night. New Yorkers remember to complain about the crowds, but forget that without the crowds New York would be Cedar Rapids.

So instead of making lists, the right approach is to reconstruct what was on your parents' minds when they were deciding whether to conceive a child. What were their biases? Is it more likely that they were undercounting costs or undercounting benefits?

They're unlikely to have overlooked many costs, because the costs are concentrated in your own family: your birth diverted resources (including tangibles like inherited land and intangibles like parental attention) away from your parents' other beloved children. In other words, these costs don't spill over. Nor is overcrowding a spillover cost, because overcrowding is voluntary.

The benefits—your ongoing contributions to the world's

stock of ideas, love, friendship, and diversity—are more diffuse. I'm glad you are around to read this book, for example (and even gladder if you paid for it!). If you build a better mousetrap, millions will be in your debt. If all you do is smile, you'll still brighten thousands of days. We don't know how to list those benefits, but we do know that a lot of them spill over onto total strangers, and your parents probably didn't think about them very much.

So when your parents were deciding whether to bring you into this world, they weighed most of the costs against only a small part of the benefits—and they *still* wanted you! From a broader social perspective—one that weighs *all* the costs and benefits—you must have been quite a bargain indeed.

The same argument applies to most children—excepting only those who impose substantial costs outside their own families by becoming thieves, conquerors, or public broadcasters.

When a decision maker is more conscious of costs than of benefits, he tends to make decisions that are overly conservative. That almost surely means that parents have fewer children than is socially desirable, and therefore the population grows too slowly.

Population growth is like pollution in reverse. The owner of a polluting steel mill weighs all its benefits (that is, his profits) against only a portion of its costs (he counts his expenses, but not the neighbors' health). Therefore he overproduces. Parents weigh all—or at least most—of the costs of an additional child (resources diverted from their other children) against only a portion of the benefits (they count their own love for their children, but not others' love for their children). Therefore they *under*produce.

To put this another way, it's always an occasion for joy when other people have more children: those children just might enrich your life, and somebody else does all the work of raising them. That means we should be willing to subsidize each other's reproduction. In the absence of those subsidies we get too few children—just as in the absence of appropriate fines or taxes we get too much pollution.

Somewhere there is a young lady whose life has been impoverished by my failure to sire the son who would someday sweep her off her feet. If I cared as much about that young lady as I do about my own daughter, I'd have produced that son. But because I acted as if other people's children are less important than my own, I stopped reproducing too soon.

In other words, I was being selfish when I limited the size of my family. I understand selfishness. But I can't understand encouraging *others* to be selfish, which is the entire purpose of organizations like Zero Population Growth (now renamed Population Connection). It would make more sense to look for ways to subsidize reproduction. A world with many people is not only a more prosperous world; it is also a world that offers more potential friends who share our interests, more small acts of kindness between strangers, and a better chance of finding love. That's the kind of world we owe our children.

THREE

WHAT I LIKE
ABOUT SCROOGE

Here's what I like about Ebenezer Scrooge: His meager lodgings were dark because darkness is cheap, and barely heated because coal is not free. His dinner was gruel, which he prepared himself. Scrooge paid no man to wait on him.

Scrooge has been called ungenerous. I say that's a bum rap. What could be more generous than keeping your lamps unlit and your plate unfilled, leaving more fuel for others to burn and more food for others to eat? Who is a more benevolent neighbor than the man who employs no servants, freeing them to wait on someone else?

Oh, it might be slightly more complicated. When Scrooge demands less coal for his fire, miners might decide to dig less coal out of the ground. But that's fine too. Now instead of digging coal for Scrooge, some would-be miner is free to perform some other service for himself or for someone else.

Dickens tells us that the Lord Mayor, in the stronghold of the mighty Mansion House, ordered his fifty cooks and butlers to keep Christmas as a Lord Mayor's household should—presumably for a houseful of guests who lavishly praised the Lord Mayor's generosity. The bricks, mortar, and labor that built the Mansion House might otherwise have built housing for hundreds; Scrooge, by living in three sparse rooms, deprived no man of a home. By employing no cooks or butlers, he ensured that cooks and butlers were available to some other household where guests reveled in ignorance of their debt to Ebenezer Scrooge.

In this whole world, there is nobody more generous than the miser—the man who could deplete the world's resources but chooses not to. The only difference between miserliness and philanthrophy is that the philanthropist serves a favored few while the miser spreads his largesse far and wide.

If you build a house but refuse to buy a house, the rest of the world is one house richer. If you earn a dollar but refuse to spend a dollar, the rest of the world is one dollar richer—because you produced a dollar's worth of goods and didn't consume them.

Who exactly gets those goods? That depends on how you save. Put a dollar in the bank and you'll bid down the interest rate by just enough so someone somewhere can afford an extra dollar's worth of vacation or home improvement. Put a dollar in your mattress and (by effectively reducing the money supply) you'll drive down prices by just enough so someone somewhere can have an extra dollar's worth of coffee with his dinner. Scrooge, no doubt a canny investor, lent his money at interest. His less conventional namesake Scrooge McDuck filled a vault with dollar bills to roll around in. No matter. Ebenezer Scrooge lowered interest rates. Scrooge McDuck lowered prices. Each Scrooge enriched his neighbors as much as any Lord Mayor who invited the town in for a Christmas meal.

* * *

This is a law of arithmetic: if Scrooge eats less, there's more food for someone else.

This is a law of economics: if nobody else wants that extra food, then something—either a price or an interest rate—has to adjust until someone wants it.

There is very little use in disputing the laws of economics and none at all in disputing the laws of arithmetic. But when I first defended Scrooge in print, there was no lack of readers who tried.

Here was their argument: Scrooge has, let's say, a chest of gold he refuses to spend. His neighbor Cuthbert is starving. But if Scrooge hires Cuthbert to wait on him, then Cuthbert gets paid in gold, which he can exchange for a turkey. So the more Scrooge spends, the more Cuthbert eats.

Here's what they overlooked: Cuthbert's turkey has to come from somewhere. It doesn't come from Scrooge, because he would never have splurged on turkey in the first place. Instead it comes from another neighbor. Call him Egmond.

What convinces Egmond to give up his turkey? That depends on the details of the local banking and commerce systems, but the most likely story is that when Cuthbert goes to buy a turkey, the store owner notices he's got more buyers than turkeys, so he raises his price—and keeps raising it until someone like Egmond walks away.

Or maybe the rising price of poultry induces Adelbert the farmer to raise more turkeys. But then the labor and feed that produce those turkeys is unavailable to raise chickens, so someone goes without a chicken.

The inescapable point is that Cuthbert's turkey can't come from nowhere, and it doesn't come from Scrooge. That means it's got to come from someone else.

One reader actually told me that "the gold Scrooge hoarded could have fed the coal miner's starving children." No, actually it couldn't have. Gold is rather low in protein, carbohydrates, fat, and other essential nutrients (though it might be an excellent source of fiber). You can trade gold for food, but then someone else eats less. My reader, oblivious to these realities, berated Scrooge for "removing capital from the economy and starving those who would have benefited from its movement." Removing capital from the economy! Let this be an object lesson in the perils of throwing around buzzwords without stopping to think about what's actually going on.

Was Scrooge unpalatable? Yes. He never cared a bit that his self-denial left more for others. But it *did* leave more for others, which is what matters after all.

Was Scrooge selfish? Surely not. He was miserly, which is a different thing altogether. Selfishness is all about claiming a bigger share of the world's resources; miserliness is all about claiming a smaller one. There is no such thing as a selfish miser.

Was Scrooge uncharitable? Yes and no. Charity means consuming less so others can have more. But Scrooge already consumed so minimally that he'd maxed out his capacity for charity. If he wasn't planning to eat anyway, then any food he gave the Cratchits would come out of someone else's mouth, not his own.

In 1848, gold was discovered at Sutter's Mill near San Francisco. Over the next several years, as many as three hundred thousand Gold Rushers—mostly young ambitious men—migrated west to seek their fortunes. This was at a time when there were only three million adult men under 40 in the entire country.

For as long as they were digging in the gold mines, every one of those young ambitious men was unavailable to work a farm, manage a grocery store, or start a business. As a drain on the economy, the California Gold Rush was the equivalent of a major foreign war.

Some miners made fortunes, but no miner was socially productive. At best, they found a lot of gold, but gold has almost no social value. My correspondent notwithstanding, nobody, not even a starving child, can eat it. There aren't many other productive things you can do with it either, except fill teeth or make pretty jewelry.

For a society to allocate so many productive workers to such an unproductive activity is nuts—almost as nuts as sending half your 18-year-olds to institutions where they can drink beer and play Frisbee for four years. At least we can afford such extravagances a little better than our nineteenth-century ancestors.

There are two ways to get rich. You can create new wealth or you can take someone else's. The miner who strikes gold creates (almost) no wealth, yet he ends up wealthy. So whose wealth is he taking?

He takes it, in tiny dribs and drabs, from everyone else who owns gold. By increasing the gold supply, he (ever so slightly) bids down the price of gold. That small loss in value, multiplied by the millions of people who own gold nuggets or gold jewelry, is the true source of the miner's wealth.

The unsuccessful miner gains nothing for himself and imposes no costs on his neighbors. The successful miner earns a fortune and costs his neighbors a collective fortune. From a social point of view (accounting for both the miner and his neighbors), both are equally miserable failures.

Today, instead of the California Gold Rush, we have Texas Hold 'Em—another potentially lucrative but socially useless activity (socially useless, that is, except insofar as players or spectators have a good time). In poker, as in gold mining, you can't win unless someone else loses. The only difference is that poker players get rich at the expense of other poker players, whereas miners get rich at the expense of people everywhere.

If 10 percent of the population played poker full-time, the world would be a much poorer place. Fortunately, that won't happen. The average poker player wins nothing, which puts a natural brake on entry to that profession. But the average miner can be quite successful, at least until a few hundred thousand of his contemporaries show up to compete with him. So gold rushes, unfortunately, can mushroom, while "poker rushes" are at least self-limiting. But each is on its own scale a social disaster.

Gold sitting in a mine is like gold sitting in a vault—it's harmless till someone digs it out and starts spending it.

Mining is a lot like pollution—it takes harmless substances and transforms them into something harmful—harmful, that is, to everyone who suffers when prices rise. (In fact, mining's probably worse than pollution; at least pollution is usually a by-product of something useful.) It's smart to discourage that kind of activity. Gold mining should probably have been taxed out of existence a couple of centuries ago.

But a miser is the mirror image of a miner—what the miner digs up, the miser (at least figuratively, and sometimes literally) buries right back in the ground. So if miners should be taxed, then misers should be subsidized.

Saving *is* philanthropy, and the tax system should recognize as much. If there's a tax deduction for charitable giving, there should be a tax deduction for saving. What you earn and don't spend is your contribution to the world, and it's equally a contribution whether you give it away or squirrel it away.

Of course, there's always the threat that some meddling ghosts will come along and convince you to deplete your savings, at which point it makes sense (insofar as the taxation of income ever makes sense) to start taxing you. Which is exactly what Individual Retirement Accounts are all about: they shield your earnings from taxation for as long as you save (that is, for as long as you let others enjoy the fruits of your labor), but no longer.

Great artists are sometimes unaware of the deepest meanings in their own creations. Though Dickens might not have recognized it, the primary moral of *A Christmas Carol* is that there should be no limit on IRA contributions. This is quite independent of all the other reasons why the tax system should encourage saving (e.g., the salutary effects on economic growth).

If Christmas is the season of selflessness, then surely one of the great symbols of Christmas should be Ebenezer Scrooge— the old Scrooge, not the reformed one. It's taxes, not misers, that need reforming.

FOUR
WHO'S THE FAIREST
OF THEM ALL?

"I know what wages beauty gives," declared the poet William Butler Yeats. Modern econometricians know more precisely. After controlling for education and experience, beautiful people—that is, people who are rated "beautiful" by panelists judging arrays of photographs—earn about 5 percent more than the rest of us.

As beauty is rewarded, so ugliness is penalized. Ugly women earn about 5 percent less than ordinary women, and ugly men earn about 10 percent less than ordinary men. That's right: the market punishes men more severely than women for being unattractive.

Partly, that's because ugly women tend to opt out of the labor market entirely, so they don't get counted in the statistics. In fact, the ugliest married women (those who are rated in the lowest 6 percent lookswise) are 8 percent less likely to look for a job than other women. That's a pretty big effect, but it's only big enough to explain a fraction of the gender gap in wages.

And men's looks haunt them at every stage of their careers. Better-looking men get more job offers, higher starting salaries, and better raises. For women, good looks command better raises but usually not better job offers or starting salaries.

Not that women have it easy. Ugly women might not suffer as much in the labor market as ugly men, but they fare far worse in the marriage market. The ugliest women attract the lowest-quality husbands (as measured by educational achievement or earnings potential). The effect is not symmetric, though: the most beautiful women do no better than average on the marriage market. For men, looks don't seem to affect marriage prospects at all.

And even in the labor market, where men suffer more for being ugly, it's women—and specifically white women—who suffer more for being fat. An extra sixty-five pounds typically cost a white woman 7 percent of her wages. To put this another way, if you're a seriously overweight white woman, losing sixty-five pounds is likely to pay off as well as an extra year of college or three extra years of work experience. For men and for black women, weight has no measurable effect on wages.

None of this proves that attractiveness (or a slim figure) *causes* success. Maybe it's the other way around. High earners can afford better cosmetics, health care, and plastic surgery; they also have higher self-esteem, which can lead to better grooming and eating habits.

But these effects seem likely to be small, for a couple of reasons. First, despite what the marketers would like you to believe, there's a limit to what cosmetics can accomplish. Second, the correlation between wages and beauty is strongest among the young—the age group least likely to have enjoyed the benefits of health care and plastic surgery.

Even so, it doesn't follow that attractiveness causes success;

maybe some third factor—like good genes or a good upbringing—causes both. But the correlation between success and beauty persists even after you control for family background, so this story also seems unlikely.

The bottom line, then, is that attractiveness probably *does* cause success. And some of the reasons are obvious. For starters, certain high-paying occupations (like "fashion model" or "romantic lead") are closed to all but the most beautiful. But that can't explain why beautiful auto mechanics earn more than plain-looking auto mechanics and beautiful teachers earn more than plain-looking teachers.

Maybe it's just that employers pay a premium for attractive workers because—well, because they like looking at attractive workers. But if that were true, we'd expect to find pretty people being lured into all occupations equally. Instead, they're concentrated in retail sales and other jobs with a lot of customer contact. Go into your local Home Depot and check out the average attractiveness of the cashiers versus, say, the warehouse workers. Or come to my local supermarket, where the cashiers are so pretty that one of my colleagues says he knows why they call it the "checkout counter." Apparently, employers hire attractive workers not for their own aesthetic pleasure so much as for their customers'.

Pretty is good, but tall is even better. If you're six feet tall, you probably earn about $6,000 more per year than the equally qualified 5-foot-6-inch shrimp in the next office. In general, an extra inch of height adds roughly an extra $1,000 a year in wages, after controlling for education and experience. That makes height as important as race or gender as a determinant of wages. The height premium affects women about as much as men. Even among female identical twins (whose heights can differ more than you might expect), the taller sister earns, on average, substantially more than the shorter.

Height matters not just for wages but for ascension to leadership roles. When I served on the board of directors of a midsized corporation, I missed half the sights on the plant tours because I couldn't see over the heads of my colleagues—all of whom, unlike me, had had considerable success in the world of business. Of forty-three American presidents, only five have been more than a smidgen below average height, and the last of those was Benjamin Harrison, elected in 1888. (Another three, most recently Jimmy Carter, were just a hair below average.) Most presidents have been several inches above the norm for their times, with the five tallest being Abraham Lincoln, Lyndon Johnson, Bill Clinton, Thomas Jefferson, and Franklin Roosevelt—suggesting, incidentally, that height predicts not just electoral success but perhaps also a propensity to subvert the Constitution. (This statistical anomaly works in the other direction as well; the shortest of American presidents was James Madison, who largely *wrote* the Constitution.)

In his best-selling and generally quite marvelous book *Blink*, Malcolm Gladwell explains that "we see a tall person and we swoon"—in other words, tall people earn more because we discriminate in their favor. As it happens, that's dead wrong. Discrimination has nothing to do with it.

You might think it's impossible to know that, but we know it nevertheless, thanks to a clever team of economists at the University of Pennsylvania who uncovered the key piece of evidence: tall men who were short in high school earn like short men, while short men who were tall (for their age) in high school earn like tall men.

That pretty much rules out discrimination as an explanation for wage differences. It's hard to imagine how or why employers could discriminate in favor of past height. If tall adolescents—even those who stop growing prematurely—grow up to be highly paid workers, it must be because they've got some other trait that employers value—like self-esteem. Tall high-school kids learn to think of themselves as leaders, and that habit of thought persists even when the kids stop growing.

Why should adolescent self-esteem be so significant? Partly, perhaps, because self-esteem, once learned, lasts a lifetime. But partly also because a kid with self-esteem is more likely to join the teams, clubs, and social groups where he learns to interact with people. And that participation is clearly valuable. The Penn economists report that "after controlling for age, height, region, and family background, participation in athletics is associated with an 11.4 percent increase in adult wages, and participation in every club other than athletics is associated with a 5.1 percent increase in wages." These effects account for part, but not all, of the wage premium for adolescent height.

Or the causality might run backward: maybe it's not self-esteem that gets you to go out for the chess club, but success in the chess club that breeds self-esteem. What we do know is that shorter kids tend to avoid extracurricular activities, and those activities are clearly associated with success in later life.

Did Lincoln free the slaves and Clinton lie to the grand jury because they learned in adolescence that they could dominate others through their height? Perhaps. But self-confidence isn't the only advantage that comes with height. Intelligence is another.

Tall people are smarter (on average, of course). We've known this for years, from multiple studies at every age level. Even tall preschoolers score higher than their classmates on standardized tests. Unless the standardized tests ask a lot of questions about what you saw at the Independence Day parade, this probably means the tall kids are smarter. Recently, two very smart (and fairly tall) Princeton economists have argued that these differences in intelligence might be strong enough to fully explain the height/wage correlation.

If it's all about brains, then why does adolescent height predict wages better than adult height? Because, say the Princeton economists, adolescent height predicts intelligence better than adult height. Smarter people are not only taller; they have their growth spurts earlier. If you were 5'4" at 16 and six feet tall at 33, you're probably not as smart as someone who was already six feet tall at 16 and then stopped growing. Plausibly, that's the entire reason you earn less.

Beautiful people get the best jobs, the best mates, and the most attention, leaving the dregs for you and me. On the other hand, beautiful people are sure nice to look at. So you might feel a certain ambivalence when a particularly beautiful person enters the communal visual stream. In the end, other people's beauty could be either a blessing or a curse.

Or maybe you feel no ambivalence at all. When Veronica shows up at the ball dressed to kill, Archie is delighted and Betty is dejected, but nobody is ambivalent.

After netting out the benefits to Archie and the costs to Betty, Veronica's self-beautification efforts might either cleanse or pollute the communal stream. If the former, you could argue for subsidizing beauty (either directly, with cash handouts to the best-looking people in the public square, or indirectly with tax breaks for cosmetics and plastic surgery). But if the latter, then perhaps beauty (or the products that enhance it) should be discouraged through taxes.

Subsidies or taxes? The answer depends partly on what men care about, partly on what women care about, and partly on how much women differ from each other in the first place.* Here's a thought experiment: suppose women care about their looks only because each man marries the prettiest woman who will have him.† Then women with no hope of beating the competition might just as well give up. Why should Betty spend all day at the hairdresser's if she knows Veronica will still outshine her at the ball?

Now that Betty's conceded the contest to Veronica, she's got no incentive to spruce herself up. That's bad news for those of us who still have to look at her—so maybe we should subsidize beauty to improve her incentives.‡

But when women think they've got a shot at outdoing each other, we have the opposite problem. Betty gets her hair styled to outdo Veronica; Veronica gets a manicure to outdo Betty; Betty gets a face lift; Veronica goes in for liposuction. In the end, only one of them can win this arms race, though a lot of resources get spent along the way.

All along, they're conferring (spillover) benefits on Archie and (spillover) costs on each other. Depending on the size of

* There is simply no way to carry on this discussion without gender-specific examples. If you don't like the choices I've made, feel free to interchange *men* with *women* throughout.

† There is no need to send an email informing me that this example departs in important ways from reality.

‡ Or, instead of rewarding beauty, we could punish ugliness. When I entered the University of Chicago in the 1970s, a law on the books prohibited "unsightly or disgusting persons" from being seen in public places. In those days, long before it was chic to look like you lived in a library basement, a strict application of the law could easily have decimated Chicago's student body.

those costs and benefits, the net effect could be either too little beauty or too much—and hence an argument either for subsidizing beauty or for taxing it.

There's yet another consideration to throw into the mix. After Archie has already chosen Veronica, does he prefer to see Betty grow prettier or uglier? Which is more important: having lots of pretty girls to look at, or knowing that you've chosen one of the prettiest?

Betty's beautification project is costly to women she competes with, beneficial to men who catch a glimpse of her, and possibly costly to men who want to flaunt their trophy wives and girlfriends. With costs and benefits flying off in every direction, it's hard to judge what the right policy should be.

If beauty can fuel a destructive arms race then so, perhaps, can wealth, or conspicuous displays thereof. This observation, of course, is at least as old as the expression "keeping up with the Joneses." If everyone's goal is to be richer than the next guy, then you and I (like Betty and Veronica at the beauty parlor) can work ourselves to the bone in mutually frustrating efforts to be the top earner on the block.

Is that likely? It depends on what people care about—being rich, or being richer than their neighbors. If people care about wealth for its own sake, there are no communal-stream issues; we each decide how hard to work and live with the consequences. But if people care about their place in the pecking order, then your hard work and mine tend to cancel out—just like the hard work of two suburban homeowners blowing leaves onto each other's lawns.

We should also consider the possibility that relative wealth matters in the *opposite* direction—that I prefer to be the poorest guy on the block. The richer my neighbor, the better parties he'll throw—and the easier he'll be to talk into joining me for a weekend in Vegas. And the more conspicuously he displays his wealth, the less I'll have to worry about burglars at *my* house.

Most—but not all—economists have traditionally assumed that absolute wealth is of absolute importance and relative position is relatively insignificant. Noneconomists have traditionally scoffed at those assumptions. For the scoffers, it's easier to imagine being happy as a medieval nobleman than as a modern certified public accountant, even though the CPA's income (in real terms) is stratospherically higher. But when something is easy to imagine, it's often because you've failed to imagine it in sufficient detail. In this case, the missing details probably include the disease, isolation, and monotony of medieval life.

Who's right? We might learn something by comparing the price that, say, Henry Tudor paid to acquire the English monarchy with the price that, say, Nikita Khrushchev paid for a shot at the Soviet premiership. In relative terms, the prizes were similar—becoming top dog in a highly stratified society. In absolute terms, Khrushchev's prize was far greater: the output of the Soviet economy, which, pathetic as it was, far outstripped the output of Tudor England. If the relative-income hypothesis is correct, the two empires should have been about equally valuable; if the absolute-income hypothesis is correct, Khrushchev should have been willing to pay far more (probably in the form of taking greater risks along the way), and competition should have forced him to pay it.

The comparison is complicated by the difficulty of comparing Henry's risks to Khrushchev's. (Which is the greater risk—a 30 percent chance of death in battle when your life expectancy is 35, or a 20 percent chance of death in the Gulag when your life expectancy is 65?) It is also perhaps rendered irrelevant by the fact that Henry and Khrushchev were presumably men of highly atypical tastes. But it might be a place to start.

A better place to start might be with modern politicians, whose livelihood depends on pandering to the things people care about the most. And here, I think, the evidence is clear. Incumbent politicians like to boast that the economy is doing great—presumably because voters consider a rising tide to be a good thing, even when it lifts all boats.

To put this another way: if people care so much about *relative* wealth, why do politicians spend so much energy boasting about what they've done for *absolute* wealth?

Indeed, if people really cared about relative wealth, I'd expect incumbents to run around saying "Vote for me! I've been in office for four years and times are really bad!" It's true you wouldn't support a politician who held back your own progress, but presumably you already *know* something about your own progress, and you've already accounted for that in your voting behavior. By advertising that he's held everyone *else* back, the politician could only make himself more attractive to you. The fact that no politician campaigns that way is evidence against the theory that relative position matters.*

Another reason to doubt that relative wealth matters very much is that nobody subscribes to analogous theories about either leisure or risk. Do you care about the length of your vaca-

* There is a subtle distinction worth mentioning here. Even if you care about relative position, you might want to root for *future* economic progress, because the fun of getting richer outweighs the pain of seeing everyone else get richer too. But—still assuming that relative position matters—you'll always be dismayed to learn of *past* economic progress, because you already know about your own good fortune, and you can only be sorry to learn that your neighbors have shared it.

tion, or about whether your vacation is longer than your neighbor's? Do you care about how well your air bag works, or about whether you've got the best air bag in the neighborhood? In each case, surely it's the former. But if that's the way we feel about leisure and risk, why would we not feel the same way about income?

Cornell University's Robert Frank is one economist who nevertheless believes that relative wealth matters, and he's written a whole book called *Luxury Fever* to argue his case. I find *Luxury Fever* singularly unconvincing, and I once wrote a long book review explaining why.* But it contains a lot of good economic reasoning that I admire. For example, I love Professor Frank's observation that if people care about relative status in the workplace, then highly productive workers should view their less productive colleagues as a blessing and less productive workers should view their highly productive colleagues as a curse; therefore the least productive must be overpaid (otherwise they wouldn't stick around) and the most productive must be underpaid (because they're already receiving a part of their income in the form of status).

I love that observation because it's a clear, convincing, logical, and surprising consequence of a carefully stated assumption. It's also, I think, self-evidently wrong. At least in my own experience, hiring decisions tend to revolve around the question "Will this person improve our average quality?" I have never heard anybody argue for a job candidate on the grounds that he'd make the rest of us look better.

*   *   *

* My review appeared in the *Independent Review* and you can find it online at http://www.independent.org/pdf/tir/tir_04_2_landsberg.pdf (fortunately, the review itself was better copyedited than the URL).

As it happens, other researchers have brought clear, convincing logic to bear on these issues and have reached conclusions very different from Robert Frank's. My favorite example is a paper by Harold Cole, George Mailath, and Andrew Postlewaite (henceforth collectively abbreviated CMP).

Like Professor Frank, CMP hypothesize that people care about relative position. Better yet, they tell a coherent story about *why* people care: a high relative position allows you to attract a better mate. Then they work out, in careful logical detail, what life would be like in such a world. One thing they find is that the competition for mates drives most people to save *too much*, not (as Professor Frank believes) too little. Young people oversave in an effort to improve their own prospects, and old people oversave in an attempt to improve their children's prospects. If everyone could agree to save a little less, we'd all be better off: our relative mating-game scores would be unchanged but we'd all have more money to spend. And yet, while this oversaving is costly to any given generation, it enriches future generations.

When people compete by saving, the rich have a head start. So the CMP theory suggests that income inequality should grow over time. But if inequality becomes so great that people lose all hope of changing their relative positions, then the incentive to oversave disappears, and the inequality could begin to shrink.

The CMP story gets really interesting when you start tweaking its assumptions. Imagine an aristocracy where potential mates care not just about wealth but also about inherited status. The first thing to notice is that such aristocracies tend to be unsustainable. If enough rich low-status men marry poor high-status women (and vice versa)—in other words, if the whole thing degenerates into a Trollope novel—the entire social structure eventually collapses. Even poor low-status families might be able to save aggressively for several generations in order to buy their way into the aristocracy, contributing to an inevitable breakdown.

But the CMP researchers have identified a way for an aristocracy to sustain itself indefinitely. If the children of mixed (high-status–low-status) marriages are relegated to the lowest status of all, then such marriages can be effectively deterred. Then a low-status man who wants to crack the social barriers (and who cares about his offspring) must save enough to purchase high-status mates for both himself *and* his children. CMP have demonstrated that to succeed, such social rebels would have to achieve impossibly high savings rates—so the aristocracy endures.

Now here's the punch line: imagine two societies—call them Upper and Lower Slobbovia—that are identical in all the ways that economists traditionally view as important. They have identical populations. They have access to identical technologies. Their people have exactly the same preferences in all things. But in Upper Slobbovia, you attract your mate by wealth, while in Lower Slobbovia, you attract your mate by inherited status. Both traditions can be self-reinforcing and persist forever. But living standards in the two societies will diverge dramatically over time, because Upper and Lower Slobbovians face very different incentives to save—and saving is one of the twin engines of economic growth. (The other engine is technological progress, which we've assumed is the same in both societies.) Over time, Upper Slobbovians get rich while Lower Slobbovians stay poor.

The moral of the story is that cultural norms have a big influence on the way people live. Of course, everyone but economists knew this all along. But the CMP research demonstrates something genuinely new: that cultural norms can be a major influence on economic growth *even if* we adopt all the simplifying assumptions that economists like to make about human behavior.

We can go further, imagining societies where status is conferred not by pedigree but by learning, physical strength, darkness of complexion, height, or beauty. Clearly any of these societies will evolve very differently from all the others.

But what makes them different in the first place? Part of the answer, according to CMP, is that once a cultural norm is established—even for purely random reasons—it can become self-sustaining. Ideally, we'd like a coherent account of those "purely random reasons," but I'm not sure anyone knows how to think about that.

FIVE
CHILDREN AT WORK

Dr. David Livingstone, the African explorer, medical missionary, and hero of the Victorian Age, began his career at age ten, working 84-hour weeks at the local cotton mill. In other words, his was a rather typical upbringing for a British child in the 1820s.

Dr. Livingstone, we may presume, would have been rather bemused by modern American college students, with PDAs in their pockets, iPods on their hips, and $20,000-a-year educations on their résumés, gathered on campus to share a keg, toss a few Frisbees, and raise their voices in the annual spring ritual of protest against third-world child labor.

The student protesters' message to African children on the edge of starvation comes down to this: kick back, relax, and take life a little easier. That, after all, is the content of the protesters' call for trade agreements that "protect" third-world children by limiting the number of hours they can work and the environmental conditions they can work in. David Livingstone, whose childhood labor financed his medical education, and who genuinely cared about the welfare of Africans, might have advised them differently.

People in the third world are poor; they're about as poor as the English and Americans of the mid-nineteenth century. Being poor means making hard choices, such as whether to work more or to eat less. Neither alternative is terribly palatable, but it requires more than a bit of hubris to suggest that middle-class American and European demonstrators can choose more wisely than the African and Asian families who have to live with the consequences.

In fact, third worlders are making pretty much exactly the same choices that Americans and other Westerners made, back in the nineteenth century when *we* were poor: They're not worrying a whole lot about the quality of their environment and they're not spending a lot of quality time with their families. Instead, they're working long, hard, dirty hours to earn enough to eat. And they're putting their children to work, just as poor people have always done. In England in 1860, about 37 percent of 10- to 14-year-old boys were classified as "gainfully employed"— and this at a time when gainful employment often meant sixty or more hours a week. In present-day Africa, it's under 30 percent, and in India it's half that. So if anything, today's child-labor rates are low by historical standards.

There is nothing new under the sun; as times get better, children leave the labor force. In the United States between 1890 and 1930, per capita income rose by 75 percent and child labor fell by about the same percentage. In the third world, child labor has been in a steady decline since 1950, thanks partly to rising (though still abysmally low) incomes.

Why do third-world parents send their children to work in poor conditions for low wages? Are they succumbing to pressure from first-world corporations and other outsiders? Well, there were no foreign corporations in Victorian Britain and children went to work just the same. Evidently child labor is a natural response to a certain level of poverty.

If children are sent to work by parents who care about their welfare, then it's preposterously cruel for privileged Westerners, with no experience of the harsh realities of poverty, to second-guess them. And history tells us that it is parents, not outsiders, who send children to work.

The question, then, is whether third-world parents really do have their children's best interests at heart. The answer seems to be yes. Multiple studies have shown that in developing countries, most parents take their children out of the labor force as soon as they can afford to. That seems to prove that third-world parents care about their children (though admittedly it falls short of proving that they care as much as they should).

When decisions are made by people—in this case loving parents—who have to endure the consequences, there's rarely any basis to override them. This is particularly so when those who would override have exactly zero experience with similarly dire conditions. A compassionate American of 1840, with relevant experience close at hand, would have been appalled at the thought of denying Africans and Asians the right to choose.

If there's a key difference between Western historical experience and the current situation in the third world, it's this: when we were poor, nobody else was rich, so nobody could come to our rescue. Now that Indians and Africans are poor, we are rich enough to help. Some people think we're therefore morally obligated to offer that help and other people think otherwise. But wherever you stand on that issue, it surely serves no moral or practical purpose to leave third worlders in poverty and at the same time deny them the appropriate coping mechanisms.

Do Americans and Europeans have a moral duty to alleviate poverty abroad? If so, we should be shipping buckets full of cash to the third world. It would be instructive to have a thoughtful national debate on that question. But do not mistake the anti-sweatshop movement for a meaningful contributor to that debate. Closing sweatshops does not *alleviate* foreign poverty (something which would require a real sacrifice on the part of Americans); instead, it dictates foreigners' response to the hard choices that poverty demands of them. And the particular responses endorsed by the anti-sweatshop crowd—kick back, relax, keep your environment clean, and don't worry so much about where your next meal is coming from—are responses that have never worked well for poor people in the United States or anywhere else.

Forcing labor and environmental standards down people's throats does nothing to elevate them out of poverty. Instead, it forces poor people to buy a lot of rich man's toys, like clean air, clean water, and leisure time. If clean air and leisure time don't strike you as extravagant luxuries, that's because Americans—even the poorest of us—are so rich these days that we've forgotten what true poverty is like. But chances are your great-great-grandparents could have told you what it's like: when you're truly poor, you can't afford things like clean air. Nobody in 1870 America worried about the environment.

If you think you can make third worlders better off by forcing them to make first-world-style decisions about labor and the environment, why stop there? Why not require them all to buy Sony PlayStations? After all, *we* buy Sony PlayStations and it makes *us* happy. The reason, of course, is that we can afford Sony PlayStations and they can't. And ditto for the labor and environmental standards the anti-sweatshop demonstrators would impose in their arrogance.

PART II
HOW TO FIX EVERYTHING

When were you last bumped from an overbooked airplane? It used to happen all the time—until an economist named Julian Simon came up with the crazy idea of bribing passengers to give up their seats. Gone are the days when you relied on the luck of the draw to make it to your daughter's wedding.

In those same bad old days, African elephants were hunted almost to extinction. Hunting bans never had much effect against determined poachers—until Zimbabwean officials came up with the crazy idea of *giving* the elephants to rural villagers. Unlike the poachers, who would poach and then move on, the villagers know that the elephants they preserve today will still be theirs tomorrow. So unlike the poachers, the villagers harvest at a sustainable rate—and make it their business to drive the poachers away. The result? Villagers have prospered and the elephant population has soared.

This particular crazy idea came along too late for the woolly mammoth and the American buffalo, which *were* hunted to extinction (or, in the case of the buffalo, near extinction). Beef cattle, by contrast, continue to thrive, for essentially the same reason Zimbabwe's elephants survive: somebody owns them.

Both ideas are really one idea: things work out better when people feel the costs of their actions. Take my airline seat and you forgo a potential bribe; harvest an elephant today and you'll have fewer elephants tomorrow; overthin your cattle herd and you'll go bankrupt.

That's why economists almost universally applauded when the Coca-Cola Company unveiled a new vending machine that monitors the weather and charges more on hot afternoons. We weren't applauding the effects on the company's bottom line; we were applauding because this is a great way to get more Cokes into the hands of thirsty people. Vending machines run out, and they run out faster on hot days. On those days, you should be encouraged to at least consider leaving more in the machine for someone who might be thirstier. If you take my Coke away, you should feel the consequences in the form of a price that's commensurate with how much I'm likely to need that Coke.

The general public didn't see it that way, and the Coca-Cola Company eventually pulled the plug on the new machines. Apparently give-up-your-airline-seat bribes are popular because people feel like the airline is paying *them*, whereas premium Coke prices on hot days are unpopular because people feel like *they* are paying the company. But that's all a matter of how you look at it. Instead of saying "you pay a premium when it's hot," Coca-Cola could just as well have said "you get a discount when it's cold." Maybe that simple rewording would have saved a great idea.

Engineers figure out how to harness the forces of nature; economists figure out how to harness the power of incentives. Our prosperity relies on both. You can fly from New York to Tokyo on a whim partly because someone figured out how to build an airplane and partly because someone else figured out how to insure it. Your computer knows how to typeset your documents partly because someone figured out how to write the software and partly because someone else figured out how to finance a risky venture. Microsoft creates software; financiers like Michael Milken created the junk bond. Which is more important? If we take profit as a rough measure of social contribution, it's a close call. In the 1980s, at the dawn of the computer revolution, Microsoft's annual economic profit was roughly equal to Milken's annual income of $600 million.

At first, people thought selling junk bonds was as crazy as giving elephants away. The most revolutionary ideas always sound crazy until people get used to them. With that in mind, I have some ideas to share.

SIX

HOW TO FIX POLITICS

If I could make one change in the American political system, I'd give everybody two votes per election. You'd cast one vote in your own district and the other in the district of your choice. When a West Virginia senator manages to convert billions of federal tax dollars into pork for his home state, I want him to know that the suppliers of those dollars will have an opportunity to gang up against him on election day.

The problem with democracy is not that politicians kowtow to financiers and lobbyists; it's that politicians kowtow to their own constituents, spending other people's money along the way. In other words, the problem is that politicians have little incentive to consider the costs of their actions. Effective reform should supply that incentive.

So for my next reform, I'd redraw the boundaries of congressional districts according to the alphabet instead of geography. Instead of congressmen from central Delaware and northern Colorado, we'd have a congressman for everyone whose name starts with AA through AE, another for AF through AH, and so on. This would make it harder for representatives to bring home the pork. It's easy to invent a project that transfers income to a particular region, but much trickier to concoct a scheme that transfers income precisely to those people whose names happen to begin with Q.

This reform has an important side benefit: congressmen would no longer be able to maintain local offices to provide constituent services, like assistance with cutting through regulatory red tape. A lot of that red tape exists only so that politicians can win points by cutting through it.

How else could you explain the Americans with Disabilities Act? Why else would firms be required to build wheelchair ramps that nobody will ever use? Answer: so politicians can sell exemptions. Instead of building the ramp, you get your congressman to intervene with the regulators and then reward him with a contribution or window space for a campaign poster. But to keep the price of exemptions high, politicians can't give them out too liberally. So we end up with a lot of unnecessary wheelchair ramps.

In fact, the Disabilities Act practically trumpets its true purpose by requiring a large class of three-story buildings to have elevators—except when exempted by the attorney general. I imagine the attorney general makes a lot of friends that way.

Legislators demand elevators and wheelchair ramps for the same reason mobsters visit your office and do some casual damage: to remind you and your neighbors of what you're getting for your protection payments. Making it easier for racketeers to provide protection is not a good long-run solution to this problem, and making it easier for politicians to provide constituent services is not a good long-run solution to the problem of inefficient government.

By my count, the incumbent governors of at least twenty states have boasted in the past four years about how they've created thousands of new jobs by easing regulations on business. First they create the regulations that stifle economic activity; then they ease up on those regulations and take credit for the productive activity that results from their generosity. I wonder how much political allegiance the various governors have earned by granting those favors, and I wonder whether the regulations would have been as burdensome in the first place had that option not been available.

I also want federal income tax rates determined separately in each congressional district as a function of the congressman's voting record. The more spending your representative has voted for, the higher your taxes. That should solve the problem of voters who fail to keep track of what their representatives are up to.

If you're worried that this would deter congressmen from voting for spending that's genuinely in the national interest, I'm willing to exempt spending bills that pass by a supermajority of (say) 70 percent.

While we're reforming taxes, let's eliminate withholding and make all taxes due on April 15, so people can see how much government is costing them. And when I say "all taxes," I mean all taxes, including sales taxes. Instead of charging sales tax at the cash register, the store would send a copy of the receipt to the government. On April 15, you'd get a bill for your year's worth of sales tax, to be paid concurrently with one hundred percent of your income tax.

And I want those bills itemized. You'd know exactly how much you're paying for defense, how much for welfare, and how much for shoving religion down everyone's throat through the Office of Faith-Based and Community Initiatives.

Of course, the goal of all this tax reform is a better-informed voter. But that's not enough; we also need a better-*motivated* voter—that is, a voter who feels all the costs and benefits of the policies he's voting on.

Therefore, nobody over 18 should ever be allowed to vote on the drinking age. When you're 30, it's easy to support maintaining the drinking age at 21 (or raising it to 29, for that matter); you get all the benefits (fewer drunk kids on the streets) with almost none of the costs. But when you're 18, you'd get the full array of costs and benefits by lowering it: You can drink now, and then have to put up with a bunch of drunk 18-year-olds when you're 30, or you can wait a few years to drink and then not worry about drunk kids (or at least about legally drunk kids) for the rest of your life.*

That's a genuine trade-off and I don't know which way the average 18-year-old would go. But that's who should be making the decision.

Likewise, it's nuts to let 60-year-olds vote on Social Security policy. An 18-year-old kid will eventually feel all the costs and benefits of (say) expanding Social Security; his 60-year-old grandfather feels only the benefits. That makes the kid the natural policy maker.

Next, we should fix some incentives in the executive branch.

Economists have long observed that the Food and Drug

---

* This assumes that it's possible to write a law that future generations can't easily change. That's what Constitutional amendments are for.

Administration has a perverse incentive to be overly cautious about approving new drugs: when an approved prescription drug turns out to be deadly, everyone blames the FDA. By contrast, when people die because the FDA *failed* to approve a perfectly safe new drug (or because the approval was delayed, or because the costs of the approval process prevented the drug from being developed in the first place), the FDA is pretty much off the hook. If your brother dies of a rare disease that would have been easy to cure with a drug that the FDA kept off the market, you'll probably blame not the FDA but the disease.

Various empirical studies have estimated the number of lives lost due to the FDA's approval process. But you don't need numbers to tell you the incentives are screwed up, and when the incentives are screwed up the outcomes have pretty much got to be bad.

A partial solution is to pay the commissioners of the FDA not in cash but in pharmaceutical stocks. Then they'd share in both the costs *and the benefits* of bringing drugs quickly to the marketplace. It'd still be imperfect—the commissioners might disapprove Levitra just to keep the price of Viagra high—but I bet it would be better than what we've got now.

We should also pay airline regulators in airline stocks, auto-safety regulators in auto-company stocks, and the Justice Department's obscenity watchdogs in Internet stocks.

And as for the President of the United States—the president's job is to make the country a better place to live. If he's doing a good job, more people will want to live here and plan their futures here. The best measure of that is the price of land.

So we should pay the president with a diversified land portfolio—give him some seaside property in Monterey, a farm in

North Dakota, a parking lot in downtown Boston. Then he'd have no reason to unduly favor any one region. And when he's taking a stand on, say, medical marijuana use, his only financial incentive would be to make the United States a better (and hence more expensive!) place to live.

The more land the president owns, the stronger his incentive to rule wisely. Ideally, he'd own the entire country. And to get the long-term incentives right, his beloved children should inherit everything. Unfortunately, despite these advantages, hereditary monarchy has proved lacking in enough other respects that I am disinclined to recommend it.

While we're reforming the executive branch, there are several entrenched bureaucracies that should probably be reformed out of existence. The problem is that Cabinet departments like Agriculture, Commerce, and Labor have powerful constituencies that make it impossible to eliminate them one at a time. But what about eliminating them as a package?

The Agriculture Department helps farmers steal from workers and businesses; the Commerce Department helps businesses steal from farmers and workers; the Labor Department helps workers steal from farmers and businesses. With a plan to abolish all three, you could promise every American that he was losing one friend and two enemies.

That very strategy has been a great success with military-base closings. Close a single base and you've got an uproar; close enough of them at once and you've got a big enough tax saving to generate a supportive constituency. It's pretty much the only way bases ever get closed.

The proliferation of bureaucracies (or of unnecessary military bases) captures the communal-stream problem in a nutshell. Inefficient government is just like pollution—the perpetrators reap the benefits without fully accounting for the costs. Fix the incentives and the stream might run clear.

SEVEN

HOW TO FIX
THE JUSTICE SYSTEM

In 1991, during a riot in New York City, a man named Lemrick Nelson, Jr., stabbed a man named Yankel Rosenbaum to death. We know this because Mr. Nelson admitted it twelve years later—long after a jury had acquitted him and set him free.

More recently, an Indiana jury sentenced a man named Richard Alexander to seventy years in prison for a series of sexual assaults. Three years later, two other men were convicted of the same crimes on the basis of DNA evidence and a confession. By then, Richard Alexander had spent five years in prison for a crime he did not commit.

Both juries blew it. But no member of either jury will ever be punished for getting the verdict wrong.

We don't know why they blew it. Maybe they carefully assessed the evidence and made honest mistakes. Maybe the evidence was not fully presented to them. Or maybe they just weren't paying attention. All these things have been known to happen.

Overall, we'd get better verdicts if jurors felt the costs of their own inattention and sloppiness instead of allowing those costs to spill over on the rest of us. I propose that every juror who votes for acquittal should be required to house the defendant in his living room for a month—in exchange for an above-market rental rate to be paid by the court system. If you really believe the defendant is harmless, you can earn big profits by having him as a houseguest; if you're scared to have him around, your neighbors probably don't want him around either.

Okay, that's a little harsh on innocent defendants who happen to smell bad. But instead of juries, we could apply the same policy to parole boards. Unlike juries, parole boards are *supposed* to care about palatability.

For jurors, we could start with an objective written test on the trial proceedings ("True or False: the victim's neighbor said she heard a dog bark at midnight"), and reward the high scorers with cash. That would at least get them to pay attention.

Then when it comes time to deliberate, we can split the jury into two panels of six and reward them if their verdicts coincide. If there's one thing we've learned from decades of watching *The Newlywed Game,* it's that contestants who are trying to match each other's answers generally strive to answer accurately.

Or we could use the occasional Lemrick Nelson or Richard Alexander case to send jurors a message, by hitting them with a hefty fine for getting the verdict wrong. We can balance that with a hefty reward for jurors whose verdicts are subsequently vindicated by new evidence.

That way, we'd have fewer jurors falling asleep in the courtroom, ignoring evidence that takes some effort to decipher, or letting themselves be cowed in the jury room. And there's a side benefit: If there's a general sense that juries are too lenient, we can make them harsher by increasing the punishment for a false acquittal or the reward for a true conviction. If there's a general sense that juries are too harsh, we can do the opposite. That's one of the hallmarks of a good incentive system—it's easily tweaked when you want it to work a little differently.

Unfortunately, cases like Nelson's and Alexander's are probably too rare to have much impact on jurors' incentives. But we can fix that. Some cases never go to trial because the defendant's guilt or innocence is clearly established by, say, a detailed confession or an airtight alibi. I say we go ahead and try those defendants anyway, in mock trials where the confession or airtight alibi is hidden from the jury. At the end, we can penalize the jurors (and ignore the verdict) if they get it wrong, or reward them if they get it right. No juror would ever know if he's sitting on a mock trial or a real one, so there would always be an incentive to strive for accuracy.

Sound expensive? Sure, it's expensive. Maybe we'd need to run one mock trial for every four real trials; that would increase the costs of running the court system by about 25 percent. But in return, we'd not only motivate jurors to pay attention; we'd probably also attract a better class of jurors. In high-profile trials, it's not uncommon for each side to spend millions presenting its case. In that light, it doesn't seem so extravagant to spend another million dollars or so inducing the jury to consider all the evidence carefully.

In any event, whether or not mock trials are worth the cost, there's no reason we can't use the occasional Lemrick Nelson case to send jurors a message. Every assembly-line worker in America, every cabdriver, every doctor and lawyer and economist, reaps financial rewards and punishments that depend on his performance. Only jurors are excepted. You can justify that exception only if you believe getting court verdicts right is the least important job in America.

Am I serious? Of course I'm serious. Some ideas may prove more practical than others, but even the most outlandish are offered here to highlight real-world problems that somebody ought to be thinking about. When I muse about requiring jurors to bring acquitted defendants home with them, I'm really saying, "Look. As it is, jurors don't get punished for getting their verdicts wrong. We should try to think of ways to fix that." And that's dead serious.

Is it fair to punish diligent jurors who make honest mistakes? Of course not. Nor is it fair to punish diligent farmers whose crops fail or diligent authors whose books don't sell or diligent bakers who misread the market and make too many bagels. In an ideal world, we'd reward effort. In the world we live in, effort is unobservable, so we reward results.

Unfairness is part of any good incentive system. You can spend years learning the restaurant business, carefully line up your investors, your decorators and your kitchen staff, brilliantly fill a market niche—and still fail because of a stray rat, a random terrorist attack, or a sudden fad for home cooking. We accept that kind of unfairness as part of a system that encourages entrepreneurs to do the best they can with the limited information they've got, and that yields, on average, better restaurants than we could get any other way.

Anyway, if we're talking about fairness, what could be less fair than sending an innocent person to jail or setting a killer loose on the streets? If we can lessen some of that unfairness with a bit of unfairness to jurors, I'm all for it.

Besides, an incentive system would not require us to treat jurors badly. Businesses fail every day, but the prospective rewards still attract plenty of new entrepreneurs. Likewise, even if jurors were penalized for bad verdicts, we'd have a stream of volunteer jurors as long as we paid them a reasonable wage for serving in the first place. In fact, attracting volunteer jurors would have several advantages: not only would they be more capable and better motivated, but—in case anyone still cares—at least this one aspect of the court system would be brought into compliance with the Thirteenth Amendment to the Constitution.*

Another way to get better verdicts would be to stop treating jurors like children. Nowadays, we forbid them to read newspapers or discuss their deliberations with friends and family members. But during well-publicized cases—like the celebrity "trials of the century" that come along every couple of years or so—a lot of thoughtful arguments get presented, and not all of them get presented in the courtroom. Why would we want to shield jurors from perfectly good reasoning just because it happens to arise not in the courtroom but in an editorial or over the dinner table?

The standard response, of course, is that we want to shield jurors from *bad* reasoning. But why? If we trust these people to sort out bad reasoning from good reasoning in the courtroom, why would we not trust them to sort out bad reasoning from good reasoning on the editorial page?

The current system of shielding jurors from "irrelevant" in-

---

* "Neither slavery nor involuntary servitude, except as a punishment for crime whereof the party shall have been duly convicted, shall exist within the United States, or any place subject to their jurisdiction."

formation (like newspaper accounts, or a defendant's past convictions) is weirdly inconsistent. A juror who is capable of sorting through conflicting claims from dueling DNA experts is surely also capable of judging the informational content of a past conviction.

We allow judges to exclude evidence even though, once evidence has been introduced, we trust jurors to decide how much weight it should receive. In other words, we believe that jurors are perfectly competent to decide whether a given piece of evidence should be given a weight of 30 percent or 70 percent or 90 percent, but not whether that same piece of evidence should be given a weight of zero percent. I can think of no set of beliefs about the limits of jurors' competence that would recommend such a policy.

Either jurors are capable of deciding how much weight to assign to a given bit of evidence or they're not. If they are capable, then by all means show them all the evidence and let them decide what *they* think is relevant. If they are *not* capable, we need to rethink the whole idea of having juries in the first place.

Outside the courtroom, everyone recognizes that information is a good thing. If you're about to buy a house, and you hear a rumor that it's built on shifting sand, you're likely to perk up and listen. That's not to say that all rumors are true, or that you'll necessarily back out of the deal, but at least you'll probably pause for a moment, consider the source of the rumor, and weigh it against everything else you've heard and seen. And the reason you do all that is that, by and large, it helps you make better decisions.

Not always: sometimes a rumor turns out to be so far off base you'd have been better off putting your hands over your ears and shouting "YA YA YA!" But on average over time, your life tends to work out better if you listen to the things that other people are saying—at least for a moment.

But as soon as you enter a jury box, you're suddenly required to shut out the world. You're shielded from rumors, which are labeled "hearsay," and excluded from the courtroom. If despite those precautions you happen to overhear a relevant rumor anyway, the judge instructs you to ignore it. And if you do the responsible thing and try to track down the rumor's source and assess its credibility, you risk a citation for contempt of court.

Now, isn't it just as important to make good decisions in the courtroom as in the housing market? Why, then, would we exclude from the courtroom the strategies that everyone instinctively knows a wise home buyer ought to follow?

Historically, one of the main arguments in favor of free speech has been that people (on average) make better decisions when they're exposed to all the information anybody wants to throw at them. At election time, the news is rife with rumors, gossip, hearsay, and irrelevant information about the candidates. But there seems to be a general consensus that, all things considered, we get better outcomes this way than if judges were empowered to censor the news. Days before the election, someone reports that a major candidate was once arrested for drunk driving. In a courtroom, that kind of information would be suppressed. In politics, we allow partisans and journalists to air every claim and counterclaim and then invite the voters to decide what's plausible and what's relevant. Why not invite juries to do the same?

Not only are jurors kept ignorant after they've been selected, they're actually *chosen* for their ignorance. The officers of the court go to great lengths to choose "unbiased" jurors. But what is so desirable about the absence of bias—and of the informed speculation that might have led to that bias? At election time, nobody tells us to avoid the media so we can remain unbiased until we get into the voting booth. Isn't it inconsistent to prefer both a well-informed electorate and an ignorant jury?*

In 1986, Massachusetts prosecutors reportedly badgered and coerced a group of terrified preschoolers into making outrageous accusations of sexual misconduct against Gerald, Cheryl, and Violet Amirault, the proprietors of the Fells Acres Day School. Here's how one writer summarized what the children had to say:

> The children readily admitted to practicing their testimony, and much of it was quite incredible. One boy said he'd been tied to a tree in front of all the students and teachers. He also said that Cheryl had killed a dog and buried its blood in a sandbox, and that a robot threatened to kill him if he told. Another boy said that Vi killed a frog and made him eat it. (During the original interview, he said the frog quacked like a duck.) A girl claimed her wrist was slashed and it bled. She also said that a robot (like R2-D2 in *Star Wars*) threw her in circles and bit her on the arm.
>
> The prosecutors elicited testimony that the kids had been taken every day to a "secret" or "magic" room. Yet no child was ever able to show the police where this room was, nor could the police ever find such a place in spite of their diligent searching. The children could not agree upon which

---

* Sometimes, apparently, jurors are chosen not just for specific ignorance of the case but for general ignorance of the world around them. I have a friend who was excluded from a jury because he answered "yes" to the question "Do you think a man who's been arrested is more likely to be guilty than a man who hasn't been arrested?" Presumably his place was taken by another juror who really believes that the police arrest people completely at random.

floor the room was located, or even whether it was in the school or somewhere else.*

Jurors, who were kept in the dark about the prosecutors' methods, convicted all three of the Amiraults. After Gerald Amirault had served ten years of a 30- to 40-year sentence, here's what one of those jurors had to say: "I am convinced that Mr. Amirault is innocent. I think the jury was misled and did not hear all the evidence. We believed the children and did not know that their testimony was tainted . . . If I knew then what I know now from reading the newspaper, I would not have convicted Mr. Amirault." Who would dare to suggest that justice was served by shielding this juror from accounts of the prosecution's tactics?

Here's a test of your ability to assess evidence: You've just had an HIV test. The bad news is that according to the test, you're infected. The good news is that the test is wrong 5 percent of the time. So there's a 5 percent chance you're okay, right?

Wrong. There's more like an 84 percent chance you're okay. Here's why: most people—say 99 percent of your demographic group—are uninfected. So you're probably uninfected too. Even though the test is wrong only 5 percent of the time, odds are that this is one of those times.†

---

* The writer is Bob Chatelle, former chairman of the National Writers Union's Political Issues Committee.

† Why 84%? In a population of 100,000 people, we've assumed that just 1%—that is, 1000—are infected. Of the 1000 who are infected, 95% get accurate (and grim) test results. Of the 99,000 who are healthy, 5%, or 4,950, get *in*accurate results that say they're infected. That makes 950 + 4,950 = 5,900 people who got bad news, and of those 5,900, only 950, or 16%, are actually infected. The other 84% are just fine.

It's all a matter of weighing the evidence. The test result is evidence you're infected. But the fact that most people are healthy is evidence that *you're* healthy. Both bits of evidence are relevant, and it would be wrong to ignore either of them.

If you don't believe me, try a starker example: Suppose you know you have a rare gene that renders you absolutely immune to viruses. Then surely you are entitled to laugh off the results of the HIV test, no matter how dire they appear. The test cannot trump your prior information that you're uninfected. And similarly, no test can completely trump *any* prior information, including the information that most people are not sick.

The moral is that you can't assess evidence without weighing it against background knowledge—so that when judges disallow background knowledge like prior convictions, they make it more difficult for jurors to do their jobs.

Tunbridge Wells, about thirty miles from London, was, in the eighteenth century, one of the major tourist destinations in England—picturesque, cosmopolitan, a beehive of intellectual and social interactions, drawing travelers from around the globe. There were coffeehouses, bookshops, and public houses; billiards, dances and concerts; musicians, jugglers, fire-eaters, and philosophers. There was also a quietly intense Presbyterian minister named Thomas Bayes, who delighted in greeting foreign visitors. Once, while trying to describe the severity of English winters to a group of distinguished East Indians, Bayes discovered that his audience had never seen or heard of ice. He sent for a piece of ice from an icehouse, explained that it was nothing but frozen water, and melted it over a fire to demonstrate. The visitors returned to the Indies convinced they had been tricked.

Amid such diversions, Bayes wrote works on subjects like divine benevolence and the problem of evil, studied mathematics, and thought hard about the right way to compute probabilities. His greatest discovery was a formula—now called *Bayes's Law* and a mainstay of every college statistics course—that computes probabilities in light of both prior knowledge and fresh evidence. In the case of the HIV test, it's Bayes's Law that computes the 84 percent probability that you're uninfected.

Here is the essential content of Bayes's Law: everything that *can* be relevant *is* relevant. Does the defendant have a prior conviction on a similar charge? That's relevant. Does the defendant have a prior conviction on a completely unrelated charge? That's relevant too, as long as there's some statistical correlation between willingness to commit one crime and willingness to commit another. Is the defendant's brother a criminal? That's relevant, if statistics show that criminality runs in families.

The defendant's appearance is relevant, too. Jurors know this instinctively, which is why defense attorneys dress their clients in well-tailored suits and have them remove their facial piercings. Sure it's deceptive, but only partially. The fact is that not everyone is capable of looking like a stockbroker, and on average those who can are more savory than those who can't. So if the defendant looks comfortable in a suit, that's legitimate evidence in his favor, just as a "KKK" tattoo on his forehead is evidence against him.

It would be even better to give the jury both sides of the story, by letting the defense attorney and the prosecutor take turns dressing the defendant. By all means, show us how he looks in pinstripes—but let's also see how he looks bare-chested, in bandoliers, dirty camouflage trousers, and Doc Martens with red laces.

Appearance is relevant, says Bayes's Law. So is everything

else about the defendant, including, for example, his choice of attorney. If you're charged with a crime and I hear that you've hired Alan Dershowitz—a lawyer who has argued the innocence of clients from O. J. Simpson to the bomber of Pan Am Flight 103—Bayes's Law tells me to change my view of you.

Whenever someone tries to convince you of something, everyday wisdom advises you to "consider the source," and Bayes's Law confirms that wisdom. If a man like Alan Dershowitz tried to sell you a used car, you'd be rightly skeptical of his claim that he'd changed the oil every thousand miles. If the same man tries to sell you on his client's innocence, you should be equally skeptical. And if you don't realize what kind of cases Mr. Dershowitz takes, the prosecution should certainly be allowed to help you out by introducing a list of his past clients into evidence.

And this cuts both ways: if some defense attorney has a long history of evaluating evidence and accepting only those clients he genuinely believes to be innocent, the jury should know about that. It will dispose them in the defendant's favor, as well it should.

So not only should the defendant's entire past be admissible in the courtroom, so should his attorney's entire past (and, while we're at it, the prosecutor's). Surely an attorney with high moral standards is less likely to mislead the jury; why shouldn't jurors have the opportunity to assess the likelihood that they're being misled?

You wouldn't want to make the mistake of rejecting a good argument just because it comes from a disreputable source. Abraham Lincoln made this point as well as I can:

> [B]y a course of reasoning, Euclid proves that all the angles in a triangle are equal to two right angles. Euclid has

shown you how to work it out. Now, if you undertake to disprove that proposition, and to show that it is erroneous, would you prove it to be false by calling Euclid a liar?

Of course not. On the other hand, if Euclid is a well-known liar, then you might want to give his arguments a little more scrutiny, because he's more likely to have tried to slip something past you. And if he's enough of a liar, it might not be worth listening to him in the first place, because it's just too much effort to sort the wheat from the chaff.

There are only two good reasons to conceal information from a jury. First, it seems like a good idea to discourage the police from randomly breaking into people's homes looking for evidence, so we adjust their incentives by ignoring evidence that's collected without a proper warrant. I'm not entirely convinced by that argument; I don't see why we can't use fines (or even jail sentences) to discourage overzealous police officers without discarding the fruits of their overzealousness. But the exclusionary rule at least serves a purpose, even if it's a purpose that might better be served some other way. So I'll count that as one reason why we *might* want to exclude some evidence from the courtroom.

Here's the second (possibly) good reason to exclude evidence: all other things being equal, we'd rather not discourage perfectly harmless behavior by making it a liability in the courtroom. On average, people with red cars drive faster than people with blue cars. So if you're arrested for speeding, the color of your car is relevant evidence. On the other hand, if we allow that evidence to be used against you, you're more likely to buy a blue car in the first place. That's a bad outcome if your favorite color is red.

Likewise, if your politics or your religion or the cobra tattooed on your chest makes you statistically more likely to beat up old women and steal their purses, and if prosecutors are allowed to use those statistics against you in a courtroom, then you might choose to avoid politics, religion, and tattoo parlors—just in case you're ever falsely accused of purse snatching. In a society that values diversity, that's an argument against letting prosecutors attack the defendant's politics or religion.

On the other hand, we can still safely let prosecutors attack the defendant's race or gender, because race and gender are not objects of choice. It's not like we have to worry that if your race can be used against you in a courtroom, we'll discourage people from becoming black. (Though I suppose that if you carried this line of reasoning far enough, you might worry about discouraging blacks from having children.) Ditto for gender: males are more crime-prone than females, but I have never met a transsexual whose sex change was motivated by concern about being falsely arrested for burglary.

It's also not an argument for excluding testimony about behavior that really *ought* to be discouraged. If, as I advocated earlier, we allow testimony about the defense attorney's history of representing sleazy clients, it will become harder for sleazy clients to hire an attorney. Good.

There's a third argument for suppressing evidence, but I think we can safely dismiss it. Some evidence is embarrassing, and it's argued that we should sometimes suppress that evidence because it's not nice to embarrass people. That's why we don't force rape victims—or alleged rape victims—to testify about their sex lives. But it seems to me that rather than exclude such testimony entirely, we could let the jury hear it in secret, without releasing it to the public.

After all, before evidence can be excluded, it's got to be examined by a judge—so *someone* has to see it. I don't see how it's substantially more embarrassing to have your sex life dissected in front of twelve strangers on a jury than to have it dissected in front of one stranger on the judge's bench.

Bayes's Law tells us that the accuser's sex life really is relevant evidence, especially if the defendant claims the alleged "rape" was actually consensual sex. All else being equal, a thirty-year-old virgin is less likely to consent to sex with a stranger than, say, a thirty-year-old porn star. That bolsters the credibility of the virgin relative to the porn star; so by the inexorable laws of logic, it must lower the credibility of the porn star relative to the virgin.

(Of course, all else never *is* equal; maybe the virgin is a notorious liar and the porn star is famous for her honesty. That's relevant too, and the jury should know about it.)

In 1997, a Columbia graduate student named Oliver Jovanovic had the misfortune to strike up an email correspondence with one "Madame X," a Barnard undergraduate who boasted of her enthusiasm for sadomasochistic sex. They met, and then she accused Jovanovic of holding her prisoner and sexually abusing her against her will.

If the jury had seen the email, Madame X might have been embarrassed. If they had seen the evidence that she was a cheerful participant in sadomasochistic activities both before and after her encounter with Jovanovic, she might have been more embarrassed still. And just think how embarrassed she'd have been if the jury had been told about her reported past history of making false accusations of sexual abuse! Fortunately for Madame X, Judge William Wetzel spared her feelings by barring all this evidence from the courtroom. Oliver Jovanovic was sent to jail by a grossly underinformed jury but at least Madame X was not embarrassed. He spent twenty months in prison and his family spent half a million dollars in legal fees before his conviction was overturned.

Like the Amirault family in Massachusetts, Mr. Jovanovic had his life ruined by a verdict that could never have been reached by a well-informed and reasonable jury. There's no guarantee that juries will always be reasonable, but at least we can strive to keep them well-informed.

It all comes down to trusting the jury. If you think juries aren't trustworthy, the solution is not to handicap them; it's to abolish them.

Another alternative, if you don't trust the juries we have now, is to use professional juries, as in some European countries. That system has an added advantage: in complicated cases involving, say, medical malpractice or antitrust law, both sides call expert witnesses who give the jury a time-consuming and expensive education in the basics of the subject. Professional juries wouldn't need to be reeducated with each new trial.

Why do we ask jurors to tackle some hard problems while forbidding them even to think about others? Either we have a very muddled view of what jurors can accomplish, or the system has been constructed to serve the special interests of lawyers, judges, and others who thrive on confusion—as when lawyers build appeals around the slightest perturbation of the jury rituals, or when judges make themselves necessary by applying arcane rules of evidence.

The judge who instructs the jury to ignore everything they've heard outside the courtroom is the judicial equivalent of the union electrician who won't let anyone else flip a light switch. If people started flipping their own light switches, there would be fewer jobs for electricians; if jurors started gathering their own information, there would be fewer jobs for judges.

Economic theory predicts that special interest groups will try to manipulate the rules of the workplace to make themselves indispensable. Everybody knows about union featherbedding, and everybody knows about complex legislation—written by lawyers—which only lawyers can interpret. But it seems to have escaped popular notice that judges have developed the arcane rules of evidence that keep judges in demand.

You might think that without judges to control the flow of evidence, jurors would drown in a sea of irrelevant information—and trials would go on forever. But that problem can be solved most efficiently by having lawyers pay (in cash) for excessive use of courtroom time. Assuming juries are capable of telling a good argument from a bad one (and as I've said, if we drop that assumption we might as well drop the jury system), lawyers will have little to gain from buying time to mount irrelevant sideshows.

The goal is to get everyone's incentives right. For jurors, this means a system of rewards and punishments for good and bad verdicts. For judges, it means breaking the judicial monopoly on deciding what's relevant. For lawyers, it means, among other things, charging for courtroom time so they don't waste time trying to snow the jury.

And let's not forget the incentives that are the entire purpose of the criminal justice system: the incentives (or rather disincentives) that we're trying to create for criminal behavior.

Criminals, by and large, must be risk lovers; otherwise

they'd be car-wash attendants instead of criminals. Lottery players, by and large, must be risk lovers; otherwise they'd buy Treasury bonds instead of lottery tickets. You might be tempted to conclude that criminals and lottery players are often the same people. That's probably the wrong conclusion. After all, risk lovers enjoy having all their eggs in one basket, which suggests they should pursue either crime or the lottery, but not both.

Still, if you want to understand what attracts people to crime, it pays to understand what attracts people to risky activities more generally, so it pays to understand what attracts people to the lottery.

Lotteries are attractive when they offer either big prizes or (relatively) good odds. If you're running a lottery and you're going to pay out $10 million, you can offer a single $10 million-jackpot or you can offer ten prizes of $1 million each. Which is more appealing to the players? Usually, the former. For the most part, lottery players prefer a small chance of a big payout to a bigger chance of a smaller payout. That's because the people who prefer a bigger chance of a smaller payout are buying certificates of deposit, not lottery tickets. So if you want to make the lottery more attractive, it's better to double the size of the jackpot than to double the number of winners.

More precisely, doubling the number of winners makes the lottery more attractive to the sort of person who never buys lottery tickets anyway, while doubling the jackpot makes it more attractive to the sort of person who might actually be tempted to play.

What's true of the lottery should be true of the racetrack, where my gambling consultant Maury Wolff confirms that complicated bets like trifectas, which offer a very small chance of a very large prize, tend to generate the most action per dollar's worth of prize money (and hence the most profit for the track). Why, then, do tracks continue to offer two-dollar bets? According to Wolff, it's because the trifecta winner takes his money and goes home, while the two-dollar winner plows his winnings back into the next race. That sets up an interesting trade-off for the track owners, though it's tangential to the main point, which is that gamblers like big prizes and long odds.*

Now let's apply the same reasoning to criminal deterrence. For the most part, criminals prefer a small chance of a big punishment to a big chance of a small punishment. That's because the people who prefer a big chance of a small punishment go into punishing careers like construction work or coal mining instead of crime. So if you want to make crime less attractive to criminals, it's better to double the odds of conviction than to double the severity of the punishment.

Add 10 percent to the length of the average jail sentence and crime will fall. Add 10 percent to the conviction rate instead and crime will fall even further. Like any risk lovers, criminals are out to beat the odds, so they get particularly demoralized when the odds turn against them.

If punishments failed to deter crime, there would be little point in administering them. Fortunately, deterrence works. Take capital punishment, for example. I am astonished by how often I hear politicians repeat the untruth that there is no evidence for the deterrent effect of capital punishment. It's true that there's no evidence for the deterrent effect of *enacting* a death penalty. But *enforcing* a death penalty is a different matter entirely. For thirty years, the economics journals have been publishing evidence for large deterrent effects—on the order of anywhere from eight to

---

* Also tangentially, Wolff asked me whether there's something inherently corrupt about a system where lotteries are used to fund school systems, which then have an incentive to produce the kind of students who will go out and play the lottery.

twenty-four murders prevented by each execution—when death penalties are actually enforced.*

Here the pioneer is Professor Isaac Ehrlich, who, in the mid-1970s, initiated the use of sophisticated statistical techniques to measure deterrent effects of conviction and punishment. Together with Professor Zhiqiang Liu, Ehrlich has recently revisited the subject, refuting his most vocal critics and offering new evidence in support of his original conclusion: Increase the number of convictions by 1 percent and (to a very rough approximation) the murder rate falls by about 1 percent. Increase the number of executions by 1 percent (which amounts to increasing the severity of the average punishment) and (again to a very rough approximation) the murder rate falls by about half a percent.† As the theory predicts, the severity of punishment matters but the conviction rate matters more.

I am grateful to Professor Ehrlich for his results because I use them in the classroom to illustrate three points that I'm always eager to drive home to my students. First, incentives matter, even to murderers. Second, economic theory predicts—and data confirm—that some incentives matter more than others. And finally, if you want to give policy advice, it's not enough to know your numbers; you've also got to know your values. Isaac Ehrlich, the man who convinced most of the economics profession that capital punishment works, is a passionate opponent of capital punishment.

---

* There's an excellent and balanced summary of the literature, with citations, at http://www.cjlf.org/deathpenalty/DPDeterrence.htm. One recent paper by Professors Lawrence Katz, Steven Levitt, and Ellen Shustorovich finds very little deterrent effect and should not be ignored, but it has to be weighed against hundreds of other articles, most of which get numbers in the 8–24 range.

† These numbers are based on evidence from the 1940s and 1950s. Capital-punishment studies tend to focus on decades with more executions and hence more data.

* * *

If we care about deterrence, we have to face a fundamental economic reality: many criminals are underpunished because other criminals are overpunished.

In a world with a finite amount of prison space, long sentences take one criminal off the street at the expense of freeing another. If Benny the Burglar occupies a cell for five years, there may be no room for Manny the Mugger. But the district attorney who gains kudos for jailing Benny is not penalized for forcing some future prosecutor to let Manny go free.

In other words, the district attorney does not bear the costs of his own decisions. His incentive is to waste prison space on check kiters, inside traders, and nonviolent drug dealers instead of the muggers, rapists, and murderers being tried in another courtroom.

Every large corporation faces the same problem. Managers, like prosecutors, grab whatever resources they can get ahold of with little regard for the costs they impose on the enterprise as a whole. The solution, in almost every case, is to give each manager a budget, so that he knows a request for thirty fax machines today will adversely affect his order for one hundred computers tomorrow.

As everyone knows, this solution is far from ideal, because managers inflate their needs when the initial budgets are allocated. But as everyone also knows, it is far superior to the alternative of allowing managers to request resources without feeling any budget constraints whatsoever.

What works in private enterprise can work in the criminal justice system. Give each prosecutor a budget of, say, 350 jail-years per month. In a given month, the prosecutor would not be allowed to request sentences totaling more than his budget.

We can add some flexibility by allowing prosecutors to "borrow" jail-years from each other and pay them back in future months.

A prosecutor who asks for a long jail sentence in one case ought to know that he does so at a cost in terms of future cases. You might argue that it is wrong to let one case affect another. I reply that one case *already* affects another because of the finite resources available to the prison system. The problem is to make the prosecutor *aware* of that cost and give him an incentive to respond to it.

Prosecutors, like jurors, judges, and criminals, are subject to a universal law of human behavior: when they're not held responsible for their actions, their actions are likely to be irresponsible. With better incentives, we can have better justice.

EIGHT

HOW TO FIX
EVERYTHING ELSE

Inventiveness is good. It should be rewarded. Monopoly power, by contrast, is bad. It should be discouraged. So what does the patent system do? It rewards inventiveness with a license to monopolize.

That's nuts. After all, making ice cream is also good and its makers should be rewarded. But nobody thinks we should reward Ben and Jerry with licenses to drive drunk. It's a good idea to reward good behavior, but it's a bad idea to sanction bad behavior, even as a reward.

Ordinarily, everyone snickers when this principle is violated. My university used to reward excellence in teaching with a lighter teaching schedule. Okay, maybe teaching fewer classes is not the exact moral equivalent of drunk driving, but the irony has a similar flavor and was not lost on anyone.

Why, then, don't we snicker at the patent system? Inventiveness is good for consumers, monopoly power is bad for consumers, and we reward inventiveness by granting seventeen years of monopoly power. Why seventeen? It's someone's idea of a compromise between too little and too much. The result is both too little *and* too much. It's too little because a seventeen-year patent is frequently worth far less than the full social value of the invention, so inventiveness is underrewarded and we don't get enough of it. It's too much because *any* gratuitously granted monopoly power is too much.

The solution, clearly, is to reward successful inventors the same way we reward successful salesmen or successful baseball players: by paying for performance, not with monopoly power but with cash. But who should pay? Barry Bonds is paid, ultimately, by the fans who buy tickets, which makes sense because the fans enjoy watching him. But who should have paid Thomas Edison?

A plausible answer is: the people who enjoy Edison's inventions, which is to say the public at large, through their elected representatives. Thus Harvard professor Michael Kremer (whom we have met before in this book) proposes that when you design a better mousetrap, you should be assigned a patent—which the government immediately purchases and places in the public domain.

There is at least one successful precedent. When Louis Daguerre invented photography in 1839, the French government purchased the patent and placed it in the public domain. But Professor Kremer seems to be the first to propose automatic patent buyouts as a matter of policy.

But what price should the government pay? How can we know what a given invention is worth? What do we do if the President's brother invents a disposable boomerang (guaranteed not to come back!) and demands a billion-dollar payout?

Professor Kremer's answer: Put each new patent up for auction. When the auction is over, flip a coin. If the coin comes up heads, the high bidder pays his bid and gets the patent. If the coin comes up tails, the government pays the high bid and gets the patent. That way, the government never pays more than some private bidder was willing to offer.

Better yet, throw a biased coin that comes up tails, say, 90 percent of the time. Then 90 percent of all patents end up in the public domain, which is not as good as a hundred percent, but far better than none at all. We do have to give the private bidders *some* hope of winning so they'll take their bidding seriously.

That's fine, till an enterprising inventor rigs the auction by getting one of his friends to submit a wildly inflated bid. If the coin comes up tails, the government overpays; if it comes up heads, the inventor essentially buys the invention from himself and suffers no loss. To overcome this problem, Professor Kremer suggests that the high-bid auction be replaced by, say, a third-bid auction: the high bidder wins, but he (or the government) pays the third highest bid. To rig an auction like that, you'd need three ringers instead of one; still not impossible but perhaps acceptably difficult. As Benjamin Franklin observed, three can keep a secret if two are dead.

You might think inventors would grumble about settling for the third highest bid, but keep in mind that in a third-bid auction, people tend to bid higher. The third-highest bid in a third-bid auction can easily be about the same as the highest bid in a high-bid auction.

Besides, regardless of the auction rules, there's no reason the government has to pay exactly the same amount as a private winner. When the coin comes up tails the government can buy the patent for, say, 1.5 times the winning bid. Professor Kremer argues for just such an adjustment because publicly held patents are worth more than privately held patents. That's because publicly available ideas provide inspiration for the next generation of inventors.

Where would the money come from? From taxes, of course. But if the patents are priced properly, we'll get back more than we pay, through improved consumer products and lower prices. And that's not just a guess—it's a fact.

Here's how I know: patents are valuable only insofar as they allow the patent holder to jack up prices. If a patent on a new kind of mousetrap is worth $10,000, it's because the inventor thinks he can use it to squeeze that much out of us. When we pay $10,000 in tax dollars for that patent, we're only paying him what he would have extracted anyway. As taxpayers, we're $10,000 poorer, but as consumers, we're $10,000 richer. So far, we've neither gained nor lost.

But now toss in one more observation: when mousetraps are produced (and priced) competitively, we'll buy even more of them—and a lot of us will be grateful for the bargain. Those additional gains put us ahead of the game.

The real downside to Professor Kremer's proposal is this: making patents more lucrative does not encourage inventiveness generally; it encourages only a particular kind of inventiveness—the kind that tends to result in patentable inventions. And in doing so, it draws people away from other inventive activities—like figuring out how to reform the patent system.

Even now, good but unpatentable ideas are underrewarded and hence surely underproduced, which is all the more reason to be grateful when one comes along. I have a few to offer.

How to Fight Fires

I believe firefighters should be allowed to keep all the property they rescue—including your house. Since the firefighters get to collect all the swag, we won't have to pay them; in fact, we can auction off the right to be a firefighter and then use the proceeds to fund a general tax cut. That way, everyone's a winner.

Everyone can win because there's more wealth to go around; there's more wealth to go around because the incentives are right. When a firefighter decides whether it's worth the risk or the effort to save your grand piano, we want him to consider its value. What better incentive than to give him the piano? That way, the piano gets saved when it's worth saving and not when it's not, which is just the recipe for making the world a richer place.

Admittedly, there are some kinks to iron out: there really ought to be an incentive to save lives as well as pianos, and there really ought to be a disincentive for firefighters to supplement their incomes through arson. But the underlying idea is solid and not unprecedented; in fact, it underlies a fundamental principle of maritime law.

Imagine you're on a ship at sea, and the ship's in trouble. There are enough lifeboats for all the passengers, but if the ship goes down, everyone's possessions will go down with it. The only hope is to lighten the load by throwing cargo overboard.

If I save the ship by tossing your piano into the ocean, who should bear the loss? Should I have to pay for the piano? Should the passengers take up a collection for you? Or should you suffer the entire loss for bringing a piano on board in the first place?

Put me on the hook for the full cost of the piano, and I'll hesitate to toss it over as long as there's any chance for the ship to survive. Take me completely off the hook and I'll toss your piano at the slightest sign of danger. Those are both bad outcomes.

Like Goldilocks, we seek a rule that's just right—neither too harsh on me nor too forgiving. And the law provides exactly that. According to the principle of *general average,* my share of the losses is equal to my share of the enterprise.

Suppose, for example, that the ship and its cargo are worth $1 million and my belongings account for ten percent of that. Then I'm on the hook for ten percent of all the losses, no matter who does the tossing. If your $5,000 piano gets tossed over, then I owe you $500, whether it was tossed by you, me, or a mysterious stranger.

The brilliance of the general-average principle is that it gets my incentives exactly right. If I toss your piano, I get 10 percent of the benefits (because 10 percent of the cargo saved is mine), and I bear 10 percent of the costs. Because those proportions are identical, I'll want to toss your piano only if the expected benefit of tossing it exceeds the cost—which is to say that I'll want to toss it only if it *should* be tossed.

That, of course, is exactly the right incentive and we achieve it because the costs and benefits I impose on others are in perfect proportion to the costs and benefits I impose on myself. That's exactly where I'm headed with the firefighters. They bear one hundred percent of the firefighting costs so—in accordance with the principle of general average—they should reap one hundred percent of the benefits.

And incidentally, while we're reforming the firefighting system, I propose a new kind of fire alarm—one that won't operate until you insert a credit card. When you report a real fire, a reward is automatically credited to your account; when you report a false alarm, a penalty is deducted. Once again, though, we should probably go slow until we figure out how to deal with the arson-for-profit problem.

How to Fight Crime

When your neighbor installs a burglar alarm, thoughtful burglars are encouraged to choose a different target—like *your* house, for example. It's rather as if your neighbor had hired an exterminator to drive all the vermin next door.

On the other hand, if your neighbor installs video cameras that monitor the street in front of both your houses, he might be doing you a considerable favor. So the spillover effects of self-protection can be either good or bad.

Sometimes the spillover effects can be both good *and* bad. The social upside of protecting your car with a device like The Club is that it helps make car theft so unprofitable that potential thieves might seek more useful employment. The social downside is that they might seek employment as arsonists or killers for hire. And the other social downside is that existing thieves will prey more heavily on people who don't have The Club. Like me.

How refreshing, then, to discover a form of self-protection whose spillover effects are almost entirely positive: the LoJack, a hidden radio transmitter that can be activated after your car is stolen, to lead police to the thief (or, better yet, to the chop shop that employs the thief). The transmitter is hidden randomly within the car, so thieves can't easily find it and deactivate it.

The LoJack is completely hidden. There's no way to look at a car and know whether it has a LoJack installed. So unlike, say, The Club, a LoJack will never prevent your car from being stolen; it will only increase the chance of its being recovered.

But from a social point of view, the LoJack has the huge advantage of *helping* your neighbors rather than hurting them. The Club convinces thieves to steal someone else's car instead; the Lojack convinces thieves not to steal.

And it does so with remarkable effectiveness. A decade after the LoJack was introduced, economists Ian Ayres and Steven Levitt examined its effectiveness in about a dozen cities. Their task wasn't easy, because just as the prevalence of LoJacks affects auto-theft rates, so auto-theft rates affect the prevalence of LoJacks—first, because consumers buy more security equipment when theft rates are high, and second, because regulators behave differently when theft rates are high.

But after sorting all this out, Ayres and Levitt found that LoJacks do indeed have an astoundingly large effect on auto-theft rates. It turns out that a 1 percent increase in LoJack sales can reduce auto theft rates by 20 percent or more.*

What's becoming of all those car thieves? Are they moving to other cities, or are they becoming house burglars, or are they turning into socially useful citizens? Ayres and Levitt examined these difficult questions also, and their bottom-line conclusion is that LoJacks really do *prevent* a lot of crime, rather than just moving it to other venues.

In fact, although it costs only about $100 a year to have a LoJack, Ayres and Levitt estimate that each individual LoJack prevents about $1,500 a year in losses due to theft. In most cases, that $1,500 benefit accrues not to the LoJack owner, but to strangers.

That suggests that LoJacks should be heavily subsidized, just as visible security systems—like my neighbor's home burglar

* This research, which most economists consider to be among Levitt's very best work, went completely unmentioned in his best-selling book *Freakonomics*. Go figure.

alarm, or The Club—should be taxed. As always, when you're doing something that makes strangers better off, you should be encouraged to do more of it.

If we all used the same insurance company, you might expect that company to supply the appropriate subsidy. As long as your LoJack reduces the number of insurance claims, the company should be willing to pay you to install it. But with multiple insurance companies, that doesn't work so well: a company that insures only 10 percent of the populace will reap only 10 percent of the LoJack's benefits, and so will undersubsidize them.

This raises an interesting research question: Suppose the insurance industry were monopolized. On the one hand, we'd have to pay monopoly prices for insurance. On the other hand, we'd get subsidies for LoJacks (among many other things). All told, would we be better or worse off? I have no idea.

What about other forms of self-protection, like handguns or cheating on your taxes? First, guns. A number of economists, most prominently John Lott and his coauthor David Mustard, have argued that the proliferation of handguns (and more specifically the passage of right-to-carry laws) significantly reduces crime rates: more guns, less crime. Lott's work has attracted a lot of criticism, some of which is deplorably *ad hominem* and intellectually vacuous. There are also thoughtful critiques, which have generated many rounds of argument and counterargument that I won't attempt to summarize or to judge. Instead, I want to focus on this question: *assuming* that Lott is right and guns reduce crime does it follow that we should subsidize gun ownership? And the answer is: of course not. Not everything good should be subsidized; otherwise we'd subsidize everything from Hostess Ho Hos to Internet porn. Everything depends on *how* guns reduce crime.

First possibility: My carrying a gun causes criminals to give up crime and thereby protects you as well as me. Then guns are like LoJacks and I should be subsidized for carrying one.

Second possibility: My carrying a gun protects me but has no effect on you. The robber stops me on the street, I point my gun at him, and he decides to retire for the night. Then I already have ample incentive to carry a gun and there's no reason to encourage me further.

Third possibility: My carrying a gun protects me by encouraging criminals to prey on you instead. This could be perfectly consistent with an empirical finding that guns reduce crime: the robber stops me on the street, I point my gun at him, and half the time he takes the night off, while half the time he shops for a new victim. That way, guns do reduce overall crime rates, but nevertheless have bad spillover effects. Then guns are like The Club and should be taxed.

In more detail (in case you like this sort of thing): I'm happy to pay $100 for a gun that saves me from a $150 robbery loss; at the same time, this causes you (on average) a $75 loss. So I've spent $100 and you've lost $75. Adding your and my losses together, it would have been collectively cheaper for me to forgo the gun and lose $150 to the robber. So I should be discouraged from carrying the gun.

As far as tax cheating, there are, once again, multiple scenarios. Insofar as widespread cheating makes it more difficult to carry on the (sometimes insidious) business of government, cheating can be a socially beneficial activity. But insofar as the government offsets your cheating by raising my taxes, cheating becomes the moral equivalent of a burglar alarm that diverts the burglar from your house to mine.

Is it moral to install a burglar alarm or to cheat on your taxes?

That depends on what you mean by "moral," and that's a subject for a different book (probably by a different author).

How to Prevent Accidents

Every midsummer day, at approximately 6:03 PM, the setting sun makes the traffic light on my street corner essentially invisible to westbound traffic. As a result, I've gotten to know the local police officers fairly well. We meet on my front lawn every week or so, where I'm delivering water, blankets, and cell phones to the latest accident victims while the police file their reports.

It is an astonishing triumph of modern safety engineering that dozens of cars have been totaled on my front lawn (and occasionally elsewhere on my property, most spectacularly when they've been propelled right through the garage door) without a single serious personal injury. And it is an astonishing failure of the legal system that I have absolutely no incentive to step out my front door at 6:02 PM with a big red flag, directing traffic until the sun moves a little lower on the horizon.

My friend David Friedman has proposed a radical revision of accident law: when two cars collide, causing a total of (say) $10,000 worth of damage, everyone who was within a mile of the accident should be required to pay a fine of $10,000. That way, anyone who sees or expects an accident about to happen will take all cost-justified measures to prevent it (say by directing traffic or honking furiously to warn of impending danger).

I see some practical difficulties with this plan. To avoid high-accident areas, people would travel inefficiently long routes—or even cancel their trips entirely. I'm sure I'd stay at the office till long after 6:00 PM on summer days. There would be a huge disincentive to *report* an accident, and for that matter a huge incentive to bribe crash victims into denying that the accident ever happened. Enforcement would be a nightmare.

But whether or not we could make it work, Friedman's proposal serves as a great illustration of a key insight: the economic problem is to get the incentives right, and determinations of "fault" are quite irrelevant to that problem.

There's a long history of confusion on this point, going back at least to 1597 when two English farmers got into a legal scrap known as Boulston's Case. One farmer raised corn; his next-door neighbor raised corn-fed rabbits with little respect for property lines. When the farmers ended up in court, the judges issued a ruling that was reaffirmed by subsequent courts well into the twentieth century: because the rabbit farmer didn't actually own the rabbits (he merely dug burrows to lure them for trapping), he couldn't be held responsible for their behavior.

By that reasoning, I can't be held responsible when my fireworks burn down your house because I don't actually own the sparks. But none of the courts that upheld the Boulston decision was ever consistent enough to take that position. In the eyes of the law, rabbits have always called for special reasoning.

The judges' logic might have been shoddy, but it took an economist—and a very good one—to go completely off the rails. A. C. Pigou, who literally wrote the book on welfare economics (the branch of economics that studies these issues) revisited the great rabbit controversy and correctly pronounced the issue of ownership a red herring. He then pounced on a different red herring and declared it white. The right issue, said Pigou, is not ownership but *fault,* and the rabbit farmer, being at fault, should be held responsible after all.

That's wrong too, and I'll explain why in a minute. At this point, the lawyers had made one mistake and economists like

Pigou had made another. Eventually, it took a lawyer to see through the bad economics and an economist to see through the bad legal reasoning. As it happens, the lawyer and the economist were one person, the lawyer-economist (and Nobel laureate) Ronald Coase.

Here's what Coase said. First, don't lose sight of the problem: the problem is that the rabbits eat the corn. Next, don't lose sight of the cause: the rabbits eat the corn because the rabbits are near the corn. Finally, don't lose sight of the symmetry: the rabbits are near the corn to exactly the same degree that the corn is near the rabbits. Therefore both parties are equally "at fault." Remove the rabbits and you solve the problem; remove the corn and you solve the problem just as surely.

If your goal is to solve the problem as cheaply as possible (and this was explicitly Pigou's goal), it's quite irrelevant to ask who is at fault. Instead, the right question is: who can solve this problem most cheaply? Can the rabbit farmer put up a fence, or keep the rabbits in cages, or move them to a different location, or trap foxes instead of rabbits? Can the corn farmer put up a fence, or treat his corn with rabbit repellent, or move to another location, or grow melons instead of corn? To solve the problem cheaply, first figure out who's got the cheapest solution and then give him an incentive to implement it. Nothing in economic theory can tell you which of the two that is. And fault has nothing to do with it.

Pigou's great mistake was a monumental misapplication of the communal-stream principle. He saw rabbits causing spillover damage and thought it should be discouraged. But he failed to see that the spillover damage goes both ways. If my rabbits eat your corn, I've damaged you. But if you take me to court over it, then *you've* damaged *me*. Those are both spillovers. Which one is it more important to discourage? It depends on who's causing more damage.

Coase's profound observation applies to more than just rabbits. It completely revolutionized the way economists think about pollution. Let me explain.

How to Fight Pollution

One of my colleagues has a new classroom policy: he asks a question, and then calls on someone whose hand is *down*. If you don't want to be called on, all you have to do is raise your hand.

The minor benefit is that students are forced to pay at least minimal attention so they know when to raise their hands. The major benefit is that students who know the answer don't have to worry about looking like dorks by waving their hands in the air. For a lot of students—especially freshmen—that's a real deterrent. They learned in high school that academic zeal is uncool.

It would be better, of course, to fix that problem at the high-school level, say with really cool rewards for high achievers. Not necessarily rewards they'll care about: just rewards that it's *cool* to care about, so they can study hard and still look cool. ("Nah, I don't care about my grades. I'm just after that free pass to the strip club.")

Alternatively we could do a better job of separating the hard workers from the goof-offs. Starting in sixth grade, some classes get free encyclopedias, the others get free cigarettes—and you get to choose your class. That should sort everyone out pretty well.

In general, you can solve a lot of problems just by separating people. A well-segregated no-smoking section can be a great force for amity.

There's a lesson here for the communal stream. Namely: if Jack likes to dump sludge and Jill likes to swim, sometimes the best solution is to separate Jack and Jill. And sometimes the best way to do that is to encourage Jill to swim elsewhere. And sometimes the best way to do *that* is to encourage Jack to bring on the sludge, right here, and watch Jill move upstream—just as sometimes the right problem to the rabbit/corn dilemma is to move the corn.

Whoa. I've told you repeatedly in this book that defilers of communal streams should be discouraged; now I seem to be saying exactly the opposite. But I'm not. The point here is that streams don't always have to be communal, and sometimes decommunalizing is the best option.

Anyway, in the appropriate metaphorical sense, Jill is just as much a polluter as Jack is. Jack makes it hard for Jill to swim, but Jill—especially when she goes looking to the legislature for relief—makes it hard for Jack to dump sludge. If Jack should be discouraged from encroaching on Jill's environment, then Jill should be discouraged from encroaching on Jack's.

When my neighbor plays loud music, he imposes a cost on me. But when I call the police, instead of going to the park or wearing earplugs, I impose a cost on him. Which of us should be discouraged? If this were an exam question, the answer would be: "Not enough information to answer." It depends on how much my neighbor cares about his music, and it depends on how much I hate wearing earplugs.

Antipollution policies need to account for the fact that we're *all* sharing a communal stream, and costs run in both directions. There's a sense in which it's bad for me to fill the air with hydrocarbons, and a sense in which it's bad for you to stop me. Nothing in pure theory can tell us which is worse or which is more important to discourage. Every case is different. But we should never forget that sometimes the best solution is to ask the offended party to move upwind.

How to Solve the Kidney Shortage

Zell Kravinsky is a man who cares about strangers. After giving most of his $45 million fortune to charity, he became one of the few people ever to donate a kidney to a total stranger—a woman who would otherwise have died.

Kravinsky reasoned, obviously correctly, that the kidney was worth a lot more to the recipient than it was to him. So he gave it away. Anything else, he reasoned, would be murder.

Whether or not you agree with that assessment, one thing is certain: the world is rife with excess kidneys. I myself have one more than I need, and chances are, so do you. I like having a spare, but I don't like it nearly so much as a lot of kidney patients would like an opportunity to prolong their lives.

In a sane world, kidneys would be bought and sold like pork bellies. Economists have estimated that in such a world, the market price of a kidney would be somewhere around ten or fifteen thousand dollars. At that price, I wouldn't sell my own spare, but (according to the estimates) enough people would sell to fill the demand.

That, of course, would be a good thing. Frankly, I can't imagine how you can believe otherwise and be a decent human being. In this communal stream we call humanity, some of us are drowning and others are walking around with life preservers. It's an act of hideous cruelty to eliminate the one mechanism—that is, markets—that can reliably get the life preservers to those who are about to go under.

At the very least, we could waive the driver's-license fee for applicants who check the "organ donor" box. If it's tragic for people to walk around with extra kidneys they'll probably never need, it's doubly tragic for people to be buried with extra kidneys they'll *surely* never need. That's a good start, but to really solve the problem we'll probably need a full-fledged market.

If we allowed a free market in kidneys, wouldn't some sellers have regrets? Sure. Some of them will end up needing that kidney they sold, and others will end up gambling their $15,000 away. But so what? There are regretful sellers in *every* market. You might regret selling your car or your house. Does that mean we should forbid you to sell them?

To focus on regretful sellers is to commit the fallacy of counting costs while ignoring benefits—each regretful seller is balanced by a delighted buyer, not to mention all the sellers who are *not* regretful. The fact of the matter is that if Person A will surely die without a kidney, while Person B, with two healthy kidneys, has only a 1 percent chance of eventually needing both of them, then one of those kidneys really ought to gravitate to Person A.

If you're worried about poor people who can't afford $15,000 for a kidney, by all means let's encourage charities (or even the government) to cover those expenses. (Actually, I suspect that if you're going to spend money helping the poor, there are more important priorities than kidney funds, but this is a small enough expenditure that I won't put up too much of a fuss.) But don't lose sight of the big picture: each year in the United States alone, four thousand people die while waiting for kidney transplants, while 300 million healthy kidneys go mostly unused. That's nuts.

How to Fight Grade Inflation

I remember when a grade of C meant "average." Nowadays, when I turn in my students' final grades, the dean's office instructs me to treat C as the "minimum acceptable grade." This side of Lake Wobegon, we call that grade inflation.

It's a cliché that when grades are inflated they convey less information. The cliché is only half true. On the one hand, inflated grades fail to distinguish between the merely above-average and the truly superior. But on the other hand, inflated grades do a super job of distinguishing among fine gradations of weakness. When the average grade is B, the strong students are all lumped together with As, while the weak ones are sorted into Cs, Ds, and Fs.

That's still a net loss of valuable information, because employers care more about making distinctions at the top than about making distinctions at the bottom. Therefore, college degrees, which derive their value from the information they carry, become less valuable on average. Here's a quick example: Mary the A student is worth $40,000 to an employer, and Jane the B student is worth $30,000; if grade inflation makes it impossible to tell them apart, you might expect an employer to offer them $35,000 apiece. But when you can't distinguish Mary from Jane, it's harder to assign them to appropriate tasks. That lowers their average value to, say, $32,000, which is what they both get paid. Jane wins and Mary loses, but Mary's loss exceeds Jane's gain.

So should above-average students object to grade inflation? Not necessarily, because students do not live by starting salaries alone. There are advantages to living with less competitive pressure, and those advantages could more than offset the financial losses. Besides, students don't bear the full burden of those financial losses. As degrees become less valuable, colleges must cut tuition or lose enrollments. (Or, more precisely, they must sacrifice some growth in tuition or in enrollments, both of which have been rising for reasons that have nothing to do with grade inflation.) A college that can distinguish itself from the pack by maintaining high standards should be able to reap substantial rewards in the marketplace, because its degrees are worth more.

If colleges pay the price for grade inflation, why do they allow it? Partly, it's because colleges don't assign grades. Professors assign grades, and professors face perverse incentives. Being human, they tend to take a special interest in their own students and are therefore tempted to give those students a boost at the expense of the anonymous strangers who signed up for someone else's class. Besides, easy graders are more popular on campus. The costs of leniency—measured in lost reputation—are spread over the entire school, while the benefits are concentrated in the professor's own classroom. Therefore the professor is biased toward leniency. The problem, then, is in the gap between the professor's interests and the college's. Any solution must involve narrowing that gap.

That's where tenure comes in. An untenured professor is like a corporate bondholder—as long as the institution stays above water in the short run he's happy. A tenured professor is like a corporate stockholder—he has a permanent stake in the fortunes of the institution. Professors should have job security for the same reason the chairman of the Federal Reserve Board should have job security: it instills a healthy respect for the long run.

Of course, this doesn't prove that tenure is a good thing, because it obviously affects behavior in all sorts of ways that have nothing to do with grade inflation. In any event, tenure is at best a partial solution to the incentive problem, because even a tenured professor shares only a fraction of his institution's successes and failures. Let me propose some improvements.

First, college transcripts could show each professor's overall grade distribution, allowing employers to interpret each individual grade in context. Then, instead of damaging his colleagues' credibility, the easy grader would damage only his own. Second, the dean's office could assign each professor a "grade budget" consisting of a certain number of As, Bs, etc. Once you've awarded, say, 10 As, you can't award any more till next year. (To cover extraordinary circumstances, I'd be willing to allow horse-trading among professors—three As for five Bs, say—and perhaps occasional borrowing against next year's budget.)

A grade budget is not exactly the same thing as a mandatory curve, because it would allow professors the flexibility to give more high grades in one class if they're willing to give fewer in another. Still, every now and then, a professor would have four genuine A students and only three As to give out. One of those students would suffer unjustly. But the A students are precisely the ones who suffer unjustly from grade inflation. The question is not how to eliminate injustice—which is, as always, impossible—but how to minimize it.

For the individual professor, a grade budget is a stifling constraint. That doesn't make it a bad thing. Economic theory tells us that when everyone is polluting a communal stream, everyone can benefit from enforced moderation. It always hurts to be constrained, but sometimes it's worth it if your neighbors are constrained too. With grade budgets, professors would be forced to give fewer As, but the As they gave would be more valuable.

If grade budgets are such a good idea, why don't we have them? That's a question about politics, not economics, so maybe it's best directed to a different sort of expert. In cases like this, it's the economist's job to explain where we ought to be headed, and the political scientist's job to explain why we can't get there from here.

How to Shorten Waiting Lines

You spend too much time waiting in lines. That's not some vague value judgment; it's a precise economic calculation. The people in front of you are wasting your time, and none of them cares. That's a recipe for a minor disaster.

Standing in front of you in line is just like dumping leaves on your lawn or ordering dessert when you're splitting the check. Because I don't feel all the costs, I'm sure to do too much of it. If I spend half a minute drinking while ten people wait behind me, I've imposed five minutes' worth of costs on others. What are the odds my drink was really worth that much? Would I have stuck around for a drink if it had cost five minutes of my *own* time?

In principle, there's a market solution to this problem. If I'm in front of you, you can pay me to leave, or take up a collection among the people behind you and *then* pay me to leave. But you don't because the negotiations are a hassle, or because you're worried about free riders mooching off your investment, or because you don't want to look like some kind of econ geek. So you and I miss out on a mutually beneficial exchange. That's unfortunate.

Here's a different solution: Change the rules so each new arrival goes to the front of the line instead of the back. Then people near the back will give up and go home (well, actually they'd leave the line and try to reenter as newcomers, but let's suppose for the moment that we can somehow prevent that). On average, we'd spend less time waiting and we could all be happier.

If that sounds crazy, try an example. Imagine a water fountain in a city park with a steady gaggle of equally thirsty joggers running by. Each jogger looks at the line and decides whether it's worth joining. Because they're all equally thirsty, they all have the same cutoff for how long a line they'll join; let's say the cutoff is twelve. As long as there are twelve people in line, joggers run right on by. Whenever the line length falls to eleven, someone instantly joins and bumps it back up to twelve.

That's disastrous. It means the line is always at the maximum length anyone will tolerate. The people in line can't be any happier than the people who look at the line and jog on—if they *were* happier, the line length would grow even longer. Since the water fountain doesn't make anyone any happier, it might as well not be there in the first place.

But what if we send newcomers to the *front* of the line? Then—because we've assumed a steady stream of new arrivals—the second guy in line never gets to drink; by the time it's his turn, someone else will cut in front of him. So as long as someone's drinking, you might as well jog right by. But if you're lucky enough to arrive just as someone else is finishing, you immediately take his place.

That's a great outcome, because nobody ever wastes time in line. You might think it has the offsetting disadvantage that a lot of people never get to drink, but that disadvantage is an illusion. Under the traditional system there are also a lot of people who never get to drink—namely the ones who never join the line because it's too long. Under *either* system the fountain is in constant use, so either system serves exactly the same number of drinkers. The only difference is the line length.

Now let's tweak the example to make it more realistic: Suppose the newcomers arrive not in a steady stream but sporadically and unpredictably.* Then, since newcomers go to the front of the line, it's always worth stopping for a drink. But if someone

---

* Note to the terminally geeky: to make this argument precise, you'll want to assume that both the arrival times and the amount of time it takes to drink are Poisson distributed.

else comes along before you're finished, you'll get pushed back. If you get pushed back far enough, you'll leave.

That keeps the line short, which is good.* In fact, it's better than good: it's ideal. We'll always have *exactly the right line length* and here's why: Entering the line is a no-brainer. The only hard decision is whether to *leave* the line. And that decision is made by the guy at the back, who doesn't hurt anyone if he stays and doesn't help anyone if he goes.

In other words, the decision maker feels all the costs and benefits of his own actions! And that's exactly the prescription for a perfect outcome.

Now, there are a lot of assumptions here. I've assumed people have enough information to know when to bail out. That means they know both the current line length and the expected frequency of new arrivals. I've also assumed that everyone is equally thirsty; without that assumption we'd get bad outcomes when less-thirsty newcomers replace their thirstier counterparts.† And I've assumed there's a way to prevent people from leaving the end of the line and reentering at the beginning— just as the traditional system assumes there's a way to stop people from cutting in.

Those assumptions can all be tolerably well approximated in the queues for telephone customer service. Here's how it would work: You call Microsoft for help installing Windows. An initial recording announces the average frequency of calls and explains that each new call will be placed in front of yours. Every minute or so, a new recording tells you how far back in the line you've been pushed. If you hang up and call back, caller ID makes sure

* On the other hand, we wouldn't always want a line length of zero, because then the fountain might end up sitting idle.

† So if some customers are thirstier than others, the go-to-the-front system falls short of ideal. But it's probably still better than the system we've got now.

you can't get through. And for those with true emergencies (like those desperately thirsty customers at the water fountain) there can be a separate queue that you pay to join.

Sound crazy? Partly that's because you're probably not thinking about how much shorter the waiting time would be on average. It might just be crazy enough to work.

PART III

EVERYDAY ECONOMICS

If you've got a computer on your desk at work, you're probably ten to fifteen percent more productive—and therefore ten to fifteen percent better paid—than your equally well-educated friends in the same occupation.

This might surprise you, especially if your screen is so crowded with instant-message windows that you can barely find your solitaire game, but it's what the numbers show.

More than one good economist has been tempted to conclude that you can take an average schlub, give him a computer, and get another ten to fifteen percent out of him. Those economists—and others—were therefore taken aback when economists John DiNardo and Jörn-Steffen Pischke found that workers with *pencils* on their desks are *also* ten to fifteen percent more productive (and ten to fifteen percent better paid).

Nobody argues with a straight face that a pencil can increase your productivity by fifteen percent. Instead what's going on is that the most productive workers are issued pencils while their less productive colleagues are issued, say, mops. And for all we can tell—at least from the evidence I've cited here—it's the same way with computers.

The moral of the story is: don't jump to conclusions. Economics has a lot to tell us about everyday life—the way we behave in our homes and our workplaces—but even when the facts are well established, the story behind the facts can be hazy. Sometimes an intrepid researcher figures out how to clear away the haze. Other times, we're left scratching our heads. I'll start this section with a few of the head-scratchers.

NINE

GO FIGURE

For the past three decades, only one economic variable has exhibited strong steady growth year in and year out: the size of shopping carts. According to the grocery-store managers I just spoke to, today's average cart is almost three times as large as its 1975 counterpart. That's remarkable, because by 1975 the growth spurt had already been under way and apparent to economists for several years.

Actually, it was apparent first to Ralph Nader, who offered it as a prime example of how consumers are manipulated by unscrupulous capitalists. Bigger carts, according to Mr. Nader, were designed to shame consumers into bigger purchases.

Even if we accept the dubious presumption that a normal shopper would be embarrassed to have the neighbors see him roll up to the checkout line with a half-full cart, Mr. Nader's explanation lacked fundamental logic. At best it explains why carts are *big*, not why they've been *getting bigger*. As soon as some clever grocer figured out that big carts mean big purchases, cart size should have jumped up all at once, not gradually over time.

Shortly after he proposed it, Nader's story started showing up on exams in the economics department at the University of Chicago, usually attached to a question like "Explain why Mr. Nader can't be right and offer an alternative explanation that *can* be right." The professors were looking for something like this: Until recently (or what was then recently), most households had a member (usually called the "wife") whose full-time job description included a weekly shopping trip. The entry of women into the workforce changed all that, so shopping trips became less frequent and shoppers wanted to buy more per trip.

There's an old joke about the graduate student who discovers the exam questions are the same every year but the answers are always different. As the shopping-cart question grew to legendary status, students began competing to offer new and more creative solutions. Nowadays I teach a freshman honors seminar in economics, and I often throw the question out to my class on the first day. To my delight, every semester seems to turn up a good answer I haven't heard before.

For example: People are a lot wealthier now than they were thirty years ago, so they're willing to pay higher prices for the luxury of shopping in wide aisles. (Wide aisles drive up prices because they require a bigger investment in land.) Once you've got the wide aisles, you might as well have the bigger carts. (Actually, this one came not from a student, but from my father—thanks, Dad.)

Or: Houses are a lot bigger now than they were thirty years ago. That means more space in the pantry, so people can buy more food on each trip.

Or: Now that people are richer, they're more likely to cook several dishes for the same meal. Or: Now that people are busier, they're more likely to eat separately, rather than as a family, and hence to cook more meals per household per day. (Of course, this also cuts the other way—busier families are more likely to eat at restaurants.)

Or: Technological improvements have made it easier for each family member to have the food he prefers. Frozen dinners keep getting better, so a family of five is more likely than before to eat five frozen dinners than to share a single meat loaf. (Sometimes even a minor innovation can have a huge effect on purchasing habits. When packaged pies were available only in 14-inch sizes, apple was the best-selling flavor. When 7-inch pies became available, apple immediately fell to somewhere around fifth place. That's because in the old days, the whole family had to agree on a pie, and apple was everyone's second choice. Now that everyone can have his own pie, very few choose apple.)

Or: Today's credit-card shoppers can buy more per trip than the cash-constrained shoppers of the past. (That's good, but you could also argue that credit cards have the opposite effect: In the old days, you had to visit first the bank and then the grocery store, which was so inconvenient you'd do it as infrequently as possible—making huge withdrawals and correspondingly huge shopping trips. With credit cards, you can pop into the grocery store for milk and eggs whenever you need them.)

You could always call a cart manufacturer and *ask* what's going on, but I doubt you'd learn much. Surely manufacturers realize that their customers want bigger carts, but there's no reason they should know *why*.

After I mentioned the great shopping-cart riddle in a *Slate* column, I received a lot of fun email. Reader Susan Provan argued that carts need room for the kids now that there are more single mothers. Quite a few correspondents pointed to the fact that supermarkets now carry TVs, DVD players, garbage cans, and other nonfood items—presumably because today's working women don't have time to shop at six different stores.

Several readers pointed out that shoppers today are more likely to be driving, and those who are driving are more likely to be driving SUVs and minivans, which have a lot more room for shopping bags. I received particularly thoughtful email on this point from both Pamela Nadash and D. Gregg Doyle. Mr. Doyle went further: more cars require bigger parking lots; bigger parking lots require grocery stores to locate on the outskirts of town where land is cheaper; faraway grocery stores mean longer trips; longer trips inspire shoppers to stock up and shop less often.

But the prize for the best email goes to Kevin Postelwaite, who sent me eleven theories, including these: Maybe shopping carts have gotten sturdier or harder to steal, making large carts a better investment for the store. Maybe people waste a lot more food today (because we're richer now than we used to be). Maybe (again because we're richer), people are substituting purchased goods for unpurchased goods—soda and juice instead of tap water; disposable diapers instead of reusable cloth diapers. Maybe the technology of scanners has something to do with it. Maybe people used to take their kids shopping and had them push multiple carts; now that the kids are in day care, the lone adult shopper needs a single megacart.

Thus Susan Provan's theory—that people need bigger carts because they're lugging around more kids—meets Kevin Postelwaite's theory—that people need bigger carts because they're lugging around *fewer* kids!

Many of these theories stand a chance of being right. But I can also point to a lot of theories that I know are wrong. Remember that we're trying to explain not why carts are big, but why they've gotten bigger. All theories about the advantages of large carts—room for your purse, room for your kids, room for your shopping list—founder unless they are accompanied by explanations of why all that extra room is more valuable this year than in 1970.

Learning to recognize bad theories is a valuable skill. It's also a rare one. Just look at the nonsense people spout about gasoline prices.

When prices spike sharply upward, economic illiterates everywhere are quick to see evidence of collusion or monopoly power among the oil companies. In fact, big price spikes are evidence of exactly the opposite. Colluders and monopolists don't have to wait for changes in supply and demand to hike their prices; they squeeze us to the limit all year round. Sure, changes in demand and supply give them a little more leeway, so prices still fluctuate—but only a relatively small amount.

A monopolist always has price-sensitive customers—because if they're *not* price-sensitive, he'll keep raising his prices until they are. Therefore, even when market conditions change, a monopolist can rarely afford to raise prices very much. Big price fluctuations are evidence of competition. (All of this, incidentally, is standard textbook fare.)

The next time someone tells you that only collusion can account for high summer gas prices, ask him what kept gas prices lower all winter. The right answer is that they must have been constrained by competition.

The reason people get this wrong is that they're confused about the difference between a *high* price and a *rising* price—just as Ralph Nader and some of my students were confused about the difference between a *large* shopping cart and a *growing* shopping cart. I have my students think hard about shopping carts so that later on they won't say foolish things about monopoly pricing.

* * *

It's not just shopping carts that have gotten bigger. It's also the people pushing them.

Take the people of Georgia, for example. Georgia is the home state of cornbread, barbecue, peach pie, and a whole lot of really fat people—to be exact, 21.1 percent of the population is obese. Ten years ago, the cornbread, barbecue, and peach pie were all just as good as they are now, but only 9.5 percent of Georgians were obese. What changed?

Whatever changed, it changed everywhere. Obesity is famously skyrocketing in every age group, in every race, in both genders, and in every state of the Union. The most obese region in the country remains the South: four of the five most obese states are below the Mason-Dixon Line. But the spectacular recent *growth* in obesity is nationwide, led by Georgia but followed by New Mexico, Virginia, California, and Vermont. In 1991, a little over 12 percent of the country was obese; eight years later, it was almost 20 percent.

To see whether you're part of the trend, start with your height in inches, square it, and take 4.25 percent of the result. If you weigh more than that, you're obese. To see if you're merely overweight, take 3.5 percent instead of 4.25 percent.

Okay, so what's changed in the past decade or so? Well, one thing that's changed is the portion sizes at McDonald's. In 1970, McDonald's offered one size of french fries; today that size is called "small." Eventually, they introduced a new size and called it "large"; today that size is called "medium." There's a new, larger, large size, but at least until recently you didn't have to settle for that—you could always go a step beyond large and "super-size it."

So are we fatter because we're being fed more? Not so fast:

bigger portions don't necessarily translate into bigger meals. When portions were small, you could buy two orders of fries and eat them both; now that portions are enormous, you can buy one super-sized order and share it with your family. How much of that goes on? We simply have no idea.

And even if people *are* eating more fries these days, there's still a which-came-first-the-chicken-nuggets-or-the-Egg-McMuffin question: Do big meals cause obesity or does obesity cause big meals? Did McDonald's decide on a whim to fatten us up or did their market research reveal that bigger customers were demanding bigger portions? My money's on the latter. After all, McDonald's was presumably just as greedy in 1970 as it is today, so if we had wanted super sizes back then, we'd presumably have gotten them. That means we still have to figure out why people *choose* to be fatter now than in the recent past.

Well, what else has changed? Here's a thought: ten years ago, you couldn't even read a local newspaper without walking to the newsstand, or at least to the mailbox; today you can browse any major newspaper in the world from the same chair where you work, chat with friends, and do half your shopping. Did Bill Gates make us fat?

The facts suggest otherwise: obesity tends to be highest in states where computer ownership is lowest, and that's true even after you control for income. And *increases* in obesity tend to be highest in states where *increases* in computer ownership are lowest. So the evidence goes against the computer-as-instruments-of-the-devil theory. Instead, computers seem to keep us trim—maybe because they're so fascinating that we forget to eat, or maybe because we burn calories in silent rage every time the system crashes.

What about smoking habits? A lot of people have quit smoking lately, and maybe that's what's making them fat. But the numbers tell a different story. It's true that in the twenty-five states where smoking fell during the nineties, obesity rose 55 percent—but in the twenty-five states where smoking increased, obesity rose by an even greater 59 percent. Minnesota, where smoking plummeted faster than anywhere else, ranked only 38th in obesity growth. New Mexico, which led the nation in new smokers, ranked second in obesity growth.

So what else has changed? Incomes have risen, but that cuts both ways: as we get richer, we can afford more food, but we can also afford better-quality food and better-quality health clubs. On balance, there is no statistically significant correlation (in either direction) between changes in income and changes in obesity.

So what else changed? What happened in the early nineties that could have triggered an obesity epidemic? Did the advent of Rush Limbaugh make obesity stylish? Did the Americans with Disabilities Act make obesity less of a handicap in the job market?

What about this? The nineties saw not just the advent of Rush Limbaugh, but the advent of true miracle drugs like Pravachol and Lipitor that can dramatically cut your cholesterol and increase your life expectancy. With medical advances like that, who needs to be thin? Of course obesity is still bad for you—but it's not *as* bad for you as it used to be. The price of obesity (measured in health risks) is down, so rational consumers will choose more of it.

With the success of the Human Genome Project, even greater advances are just over the horizon, making obesity an even greater bargain. Today's expanding waistlines might reflect nothing more than a rational expectation of future progress against heart disease.

If you don't like that story, here's another: We are living in the era of low-fat foods. At fewer calories per serving, it makes sense to eat more servings. The net effect could be either an increase or a decrease in weight.

If a nightly scoop of Ben and Jerry's adds ten pounds to your weight, you might decide it's not worth it. But if a nightly scoop of *low-fat* ice cream adds five pounds to your weight, maybe that's an acceptable trade-off. So when low-fat ice cream comes on the market, a perfectly rational person might well decide to become fatter. Of course, other equally rational people use low-fat ice cream to become thinner. So the net effect of low-fat foods could be either a rise or a fall in overall obesity.

Anyway, that's my theory, or rather my pair of theories: the obesity epidemic is caused by some combination of medical advances and low-fat foods. I'm not sure I'm right, but it makes a lot more sense than blaming McDonald's.

Here's an odd fact: throughout the industrialized world, unemployment and home ownership go hand in hand.

In Switzerland, where about a quarter of the citizens own their homes, unemployment is only 2.9 percent. In Spain, where home ownership is three times as common, unemployment is a staggering 18.1 percent. Portugal's home ownership is midway between Switzerland's and Spain's, and unemployment is a low-to-middling 4.1 percent.

The same pattern appears whether you compare countries (like Spain and Switzerland) or smaller regions (like East Anglia and Yorkshire, or Iowa and Nevada). It appears whether you look at snapshots in time or at trends that span decades.

On average, a 10 percent increase in the rate of owner occupation is associated with a 2 percent increase in the rate of unemployment. That accounts for a substantial fraction of the world's joblessness.

Professor Andrew Oswald of the University of Warwick, who first noticed all this, believes that home ownership *causes* unemployment by tying people down geographically. The jobless home owner looks for jobs within commuting distance of his home; the jobless renter is willing to move to where the jobs are.

That theory is testable, because it predicts that home owners suffer *longer* periods of unemployment, as opposed to *more frequent* periods of unemployment. And in fact, Oswald's theory passes at least one version of that test: as home ownership has risen over the past few decades, there has been an increase in time spent unemployed but little change in the frequency of job loss.

But maybe instead the causality runs backward. Perhaps unemployment causes high rates of home ownership. My irreverent colleague Mark Bils points out that if you lose your job, you'll be spending a lot of time at home, so you'll want to buy a nice house. More plausibly, it's easy to imagine that when jobs dry up, renters move out, so only home owners remain. The other side of that coin is that booming areas tend to draw a lot of newcomers who want to rent for a while.

Or maybe home ownership and unemployment are like mistletoe and eggnog, which tend to appear in the same month without either causing the other. But then what plays the role of Christmas, the background force that causes both? The most obvious candidates are age and wealth, either of which can increase the odds of both home ownership and long-term unemployment (the young and the poor scramble harder for jobs).

My cynical colleague Alan Stockman suggests an alternative candidate, namely, the regulatory climate. He points out that where regulators run amok, they tend to disrupt the rental market and the job market simultaneously. Consider the housing market in New York City, where rental apartments are outrageously expensive. That's largely because New York housing laws make it nearly impossible to evict a bad tenant, so landlords are skittish about leasing to strangers. At the same time, labor laws make it hard to fire a bad employee, so employers are conservative in their hiring.

Or maybe the numbers themselves are wrong because of some hidden bias in the way they're collected. Maybe when you're counting the unemployed, it's easy to overlook a transient and hard to overlook a home owner.

But if Oswald is right, then much of the world's unemployment is caused by home ownership—which puts an interesting gloss on the fact that home ownership is subsidized by governments almost everywhere in the Western world.

That doesn't prove it's bad to own your own home. Unemployment might be a small price to pay for residential stability, especially when there are kids involved.

If your family moves during your school years (ages 6–15), your chance of graduating high school falls by 16 percent. The chance that you'll be "economically inactive" (out of school *and* out of work) at age 24 rises by 10 percent. And, if you are female, your chance of getting through your teens without an out-of-wedlock birth falls by 6 percent.

Once again, though, it's not clear why. Robert Haveman and Barbara Wolfe, the sociologists who reported these statistics, have found that these results persist even when you control for income, race, religion, family size, disability, and the mother's work status. So you can't explain away the facts with a simple story like "families who move tend to be poor, and poor children tend to fail." That's a long way, though, from establishing that moves cause bad outcomes. So what's the right story?

I'm not sure why kids who move do so badly in school; I'm not sure why home owners are so likely to be out of work; I'm not sure why we're getting so fat and I'm not sure why our shopping carts are so big. It's not easy to sort out causes from effects. But—as I aim to demonstrate in the next couple of chapters—it's not always impossible either.

TEN

OH NO! IT'S A GIRL!

If you want to stay married, three of the most ominous words you'll ever hear are: "It's a girl." All over the world, boys hold marriages together, and girls break them up.

An American with one daughter is nearly 5 percent more likely to divorce than an American with one son. The more daughters, the bigger the effect: the parents of three girls are almost 10 percent more likely to divorce than the parents of three boys. In Mexico and Colombia, the gap is wider; in Kenya it's wider still. In Vietnam, it's huge: parents of a girl are 25 percent more likely to divorce than parents of a boy.

Economists Gordon Dahl and Enrico Moretti gathered these numbers from over three million census observations. Correlation, of course, need not imply causation. But in this case it probably does. Here's why:

Take three million people, have them flip coins, and divide them into two groups according to how their coins land. Then the two groups will look statistically identical—same average income, same average intelligence, same average height. That's called the *law of large numbers,* and it works for two reasons—first, the sample size is huge, and second, coin flips are random.

Now do the same thing, dividing your three million people according to the gender of their last-born child. The same thing happens—parents of boys are statistically identical to parents of girls, because you've still got a huge sample size and because the sex of a child is as random as a coin flip. The two groups will have the same average financial stresses, the same average emotional distance, and the same average incidence of infidelity. All that's left to explain the difference in divorce rates is the gender of the children.

Gender ratios, unlike coin flips, are not exactly fifty-fifty (boys account for around 51 percent of births), but that's okay. It just means that one of our two enormous groups is slightly more enormous than the other. It doesn't change the fact that the two groups are statistically identical.

So in this case correlation really does imply causation—*unless* I'm wrong about gender being random. But why would it not be? Why should unhappily married people have a disproportionate number of girls? Well, maybe some third factor simultaneously affects the happiness of your marriage and the gender of your children. Okay, then, what might that third factor be?

One candidate is status. The presidents of the United States have collectively had about half again as many sons as daughters (95 to 63). Far more strikingly—because the sample size is so much larger—the people listed in *Who's Who* have, collectively, about 15 percent more sons than daughters. (For the latter statistic, I rely on the testimony of the biologist Robin Baker in his book *Sperm Wars.*)

Why do high-status parents have more sons? Presumably

because high-status sons can give you lots of grandchildren (Baker points to an emperor of Morocco with 888 children). A daughter is far more likely to give you about the average number of grandchildren. On the other side, low-status boys die childless more often than low-status girls. (On average, boys and girls have the same number of offspring—they must, because each offspring has one mother and one father. But girls are clustered around the average, while boys veer off to both extremes.)

So if you want a lot of grandchildren (and whether you want them or not, your genes do), you'll want sons if you're near the top of the status heap, but daughters if you're near the bottom.

Now: what's the mechanism to accomplish all this? One suggestion from the biologists—and one that makes good sense to an economist—is that a pregnant woman's body, in deciding how much to invest in nourishing the embryo, takes account of the parents' status and the embryo's sex. High-status mothers give more nourishment to male embryos; low-status mothers give more nourishment to female embryos; better-nourished embryos are more likely to be born alive.

Can the involuntary process of nourishing an embryo respond to conscious information about status? Sure; this kind of thing happens all the time. Sweating with fear is an involuntary process, and it's easily triggered by conscious awareness of an approaching tiger. More fundamentally, the question of how much to nourish an embryo is among the most important economic problems the female body ever faces. Why would it ignore highly relevant information when it's making such a critical decision?

So there's both some evidence and some plausibility behind the notion that high-status parents have more sons. If high-status parents are also more likely to stay married, then perhaps we have a new explanation for the divorce statistics.

Another candidate for a "third factor" is stress. In many animal species, stressed populations produce unusually more female offspring. There's even some evidence that the same is true in humans. In East Germany, during the traumatic years after the fall of Communism and the difficult transition to a market economy, unemployment reached historic highs, and so did the ratio of female births. (On the other hand, there was no comparable change in the sex ratio during the Great Depression.) If stress causes both divorce and daughters, then maybe daughters don't cause divorce.

The problem with the stress theory—and with the status theory, and with any similar theory you might concoct—is that they're arithmetically implausible. To explain even a small correlation between daughters and divorce, you'd have to make pretty extreme assumptions about the effects of stress.

For example: Suppose half of all parents are stressed, stressed parents have 55 percent girls and a 50 percent divorce rate, and unstressed parents have 45 percent girls and a 25 percent divorce rate. Those are much stronger effects (especially on the boy/girl ratio) than anyone could actually believe. Nevertheless, even with these strong assumptions, we get a 36.25 percent divorce rate among parents of boys and a 38.75 percent divorce rate among parents of girls—not a very big difference. So the stress theory just doesn't hold water.

The general point is that before you attribute a correlation to some mysterious (or nonmysterious) third factor, it's worth pulling out an envelope, flipping it over, and jotting down some numbers. If your numbers have to be ridiculous to get the result you want, you probably need a different theory.

* * *

If stress and status can't explain the numbers, we're back where we began: daughters really do cause divorce. When I reported as much in *Slate*, a distressing number of readers wrote to inform me that, evidence be damned, they would simply never believe that the children's gender could be relevant to a divorce decision. My favorite of these came from a therapist in Iowa—it would be inappropriate to mention her name, so let's just call her "Bozo the Therapist"—who took me to task for subscribing to the "archaic notion" that children *ever* have *anything* to do with divorce. Unless she's been practicing not in the state of Iowa but on the planet Iowa in some distant solar system, Bozo must win the prize for the least observant therapist in human history.

Of course children do affect divorce decisions. And to a small but nonnegligible extent, it appears that girls cause more divorces than boys do. The next question is why.

Children of divorce usually stay with the mother, so the question comes down to this: why do fathers stick around for sons when they won't stick around for daughters? (Or, alternatively, why do mothers stay married so their sons can have a father when they won't do the same for their daughters?) Do fathers prefer the company of sons? Do parents think a boy needs a male role model? Do they worry that boys cope less successfully with the emotional consequences of divorce? Or do they believe that an emotionally devastated daughter is somehow less of a tragedy than an emotionally devastated son?

Dahl and Moretti believe that boys hold marriages together because parents prefer boys. This, of course, raises the question: is it *true* that parents prefer boys? Of course we all know the answer in China, with its ongoing history of female infanticide. But what about the United States?

Here's Dahl and Moretti's first bit of evidence: divorced women with girls are substantially less likely to remarry than divorced women with boys. Not only do daughters lower the probability of remarriage; they also lower the probability that a second marriage, if it does occur, will succeed. Apparently, daughters are a liability in the remarriage market, which tells us that potential husbands prefer male stepchildren.

Or maybe not. Maybe it just tells us that mothers prefer not to expose their daughters to a potentially predatory stepfather. So while the remarriage statistics are suggestive, I'm not at all sure what they're telling us.

But there's more striking evidence, based on shotgun marriages: Take a typical unmarried couple who are expecting a child. Suppose they have an ultrasound, which more often than not reveals the child's sex. It turns out that those couples are more likely to get married if the child is a boy. Apparently, for unmarried fathers, the prospect of living with a wife and a son is more alluring than the prospect of living with a wife and a daughter.

Finally, Dahl and Moretti observe that parents of girls are quite a bit more likely to try for another child than parents of boys, which suggests that there are more parents hoping for sons than for daughters.

Once again, the effect is strong in the United States but even stronger elsewhere. In the United States, Colombia, or Kenya, a couple with three girls is about 4 percent more likely to try for another child than a couple with three boys; in Mexico it's closer to 9 percent, and in Vietnam it's 18 percent. In China, before the one-child policy was imposed in 1982, the number was an astounding 90 percent!

Although they don't mention it, there's one more bit of evidence to support the Dahl-Moretti "parents prefer boys" hypothesis: adoption agencies almost uniformly report a higher demand for girls. That's exactly what you'd expect in a world where parents prefer boys. In such a world, boys will tend to be put up for adoption when there's something seriously wrong with them, but many girls will be put up for adoption simply for being girls. So, if I'm looking to adopt a bright, healthy child, of course I'll choose a girl: I expect that among children put up for adoption, girls are on average brighter and healthier than boys. I could well make this choice even if I prefer boys to girls, as long as my preference for "bright and healthy" is stronger.

So, what's the bottom line? Dahl and Moretti are quick to acknowledge that they've found no smoking guns; if you're sufficiently clever you can probably concoct alternative explanations for everything they've observed. But they argue that the most natural way to interpret their data is that parents, on average, prefer boys to girls.

When I wrote about these issues in *Slate*, a lot of my readers refused to believe that parents prefer boys. Several offered alternative explanations of the divorce statistics, many of them rooted in evolutionary biology. The most creative of these was from reader Todd Peters: boys with low self-esteem become withdrawn and unattractive; girls with low self-esteem become promiscuous. So, if you want lots of grandchildren, you've got to raise the self-esteem of your sons (by staying married) and lower the self-esteem of your daughters (by getting divorced).

Ooookay. Here's a better try: parents could well believe that boys, more than girls, need big inheritances—either because wealth gives boys a bigger advantage in the mating competition, or because boys are more likely to do something entrepreneurial. If that's what they believe, then parents of boys will try harder than parents of girls to preserve their wealth. In particular, they'll avoid divorce, because divorce is expensive.

This theory not only explains the divorce statistics, it also explains why parents of boys are less likely to try for another child: extra children dilute the inheritance.

So while Dahl and Moretti believe that sons improve the quality of marriage, this alternative theory suggests that sons exacerbate the pain of divorce. Either way, boys hold marriages together (and therefore girls, by not being boys, cause divorce). But in the Dahl-Moretti story, a boy child is a blessing; in the inheritance story, that same boy child is a curse—or at least threatens to become a curse if the marriage starts to crumble. If that's correct, then a better title for this chapter might have been "Oh No! It's a Boy!"

ELEVEN
THE HIGH PRICE OF MOTHERHOOD

"Being a woman," said Joseph Conrad, "is a terribly difficult task, since it consists principally of dealing with men." It consists also of facing difficult trade-offs between family and career. Amalia Miller, a young economist at the University of Virginia, has thought hard about those trade-offs.

On average, a woman in her twenties will increase her lifetime earnings by 10 percent if she delays the birth of her first child by a year. Part of that is because she'll earn higher wages—about 3 percent higher—for the rest of her life; the rest is because she'll work longer hours. For college-educated women, the effects are even bigger. For professional women, the effects are bigger yet.

So if you have your first child at 24 instead of 25, you're giving up 10 percent of your lifetime earnings. The wage hit comes in two pieces. There's an immediate drop, followed by a slower rate of growth—right up to the day you retire. A 34-year-old woman with a ten-year-old child will (again on average) get smaller percentage raises on a smaller base salary than an otherwise identical woman with a nine-year-old. Surprisingly, it appears that none of these effects are mitigated by the passage of family-leave laws.

How does Professor Miller know all this? It will never do simply to compare the wages of women who gave birth at different ages. A woman who gives birth at 24 might be a different sort of person from a woman who gives birth at 25, and those differences might impact future earnings. Maybe the 24-year-old is less ambitious. Or worse yet (worse from the point of view of sorting out what's causing what), maybe the 24-year-old started her family sooner precisely *because* she already saw that her career was going badly.

So Professor Miller did something very clever. Instead of comparing random 24-year-old mothers with random 25-year-old mothers, she effectively compared 24-year-old mothers with *25-year-old mothers who had miscarried at 24*. Now you've got two groups of women, all of whom made the same choices regarding pregnancy, but some of whom had their first children delayed by an act of chance. That's a fairer comparison—and it confirms the 10 percent earnings hit.

But the comparison is still imperfect. Maybe miscarriages and low wages have a common cause—poor health, for example. To this, Professor Miller has two responses. First, it appears that most miscarriages are not health-related. Second, touché.

So Professor Miller performed the statistical equivalent of a second experiment. Let's compare 25-year-old mothers with those 24-year-old mothers who conceived while using birth control. Now you've got two groups of women, none of whom wanted to be pregnant at 24. Some became pregnant by chance, which gives us something like a controlled experiment.

Again, the experiment is imperfect. Getting pregnant while on birth control might be a symptom of carelessness, and carelessness can be a liability in the workplace. So let's try yet again. We start with a bunch of women who all report that they'd been *trying* to get pregnant since they were 23. Some succeeded at 24; others at 25. Insofar as those successes are random (or at least not caused by anything that also affects wages) we have yet a third controlled experiment.

None of these experiments—the miscarriage experiment, the birth-control experiment, and the "trying to get pregnant" experiment—is perfect, but all three point to the same conclusion. Three imperfect experiments still don't add up to one perfect experiment, but when they all give the same result, we can start to embrace that result with some confidence. In this case, the result is that early motherhood is not only *correlated* with low wages; it actually *causes* them. That's largely what good empirical economics is about—finding thoughtful and creative ways to distinguish between correlation and causation.

Whenever I write a magazine column on an empirical topic, readers send me email "explaining" that correlation and causation are not the same thing. Trust me; economists already know this. Reminding an economist that correlation does not imply causation is like reminding a chemist to be sure his test tubes are clean. Competent economists always address the causation/correlation issue, just as competent chemists always use clean test tubes. Amalia Miller happens to have done it particularly well.

PART IV

THE BIG QUESTIONS

How do we tell right from wrong, and truth from fiction? How do we decide when to save a life and when to let one go? What's the most effective way to be charitable, and the most effective way to help the poor? And what is it in human nature that leads dieters to lock their refrigerator doors?

In the remaining chapters, I hope to convince you that economic reasoning has much to contribute to all these questions, though sometimes not even an economist can give you a definitive answer.

TWELVE
GIVING YOUR ALL

Moses Maimonides was the most influential Jewish philosopher of the Middle Ages, famed among other things for declaring that charity is more worthy when it's directed toward an unknown recipient. Like much medieval thought, Maimonides' analysis strikes me as kind of . . . well, stupid. An unknown recipient could turn out to be anyone from Bill Gates to Saddam Hussein. I'd prefer to know that I've fed a starving child, thank you.

Random acts of kindness are all very well and good, but *directed* acts of kindness are a whole lot better. When I'm in a charitable mood I'd rather pick a worthy recipient than just hand ten bucks to the next guy I pass on the street.

CARE, for example, is a worthy recipient. It's a noble organization that fights starvation. It would like your support. The American Cancer Society is also a worthy recipient. It's a noble organization that fights disease. It would like your support too.

161

Here's my advice: if you're feeling very charitable, *don't* give to both of them.

Any act of charity entails a clear moral judgment. When you give $100 to CARE, you assert that CARE is worthier than the Cancer Society. If that's your honest judgment when you give your *first* $100, it ought to be your honest judgment when you give your *second* $100. Giving to the Cancer Society tomorrow means admitting you were wrong to give to CARE today.

But wait. What if you can't choose between two such worthy causes? What if you're sure that both are noble, but unsure which is nobler? What if you have no idea who will spend your funds more wisely, or you have no confidence in your ability to prioritize between cancer victims and starving children? I sympathize with all of that, but none of it lets you off the hook. Your contribution to CARE says that in your best (though quite possibly flawed) judgment, and in view of the (admittedly incomplete) information at your disposal, CARE is worthier than the Cancer Society. Sure, you might be wrong, but that's still your best guess. And if it's your best guess today, it should be your best guess tomorrow.

All right, what if you have no best guess? What if, given the limits of your ability to judge, CARE and the Cancer Society seem dead-on equally worthy? Then I suggest you flip a coin and give everything to the winner. If the two causes are equally worthy, sending $200 to either is just as good as sending $100 to each—and it will cost you just one postage stamp instead of two.

I love that argument. It is simple, it is surprising, and it has profound moral consequences. But it also leaves most people with the sense that they've somehow been tricked. The conclusion seems to defy all common sense. You wouldn't devote all your companionship to a single friend, all your leisure time to a single hobby, or all your investment portfolio to a single stock. It would be crazy to argue that if you choose steak over chicken today, you should eat steak instead of chicken every day for the rest of your life. So why is charity different?

Well, let's think about *why* you spend time with more than one friend. I look forward to spending time with my friend Joe. But afterward—after we've had a chance to catch up on old times and new—seeing Joe seems, at least temporarily, a little less urgent than before. I've made a dent in my "I miss Joe" problem, and can move on to address another problem, like "I miss Gerri."

Now, an insane zealot might cry, "Aha! Yesterday, you visited Joe, thereby revealing that in your best judgment, time with Joe is more important than time with Gerri. Today, you're repudiating that judgment!" But I have a perfectly good response to that insane zealotry: time with Joe is less urgent now than it was yesterday, because we've *had* some time together.

The same response applies to leisure activities and financial investments. It's a bad idea to spend all your leisure time playing golf; you'll probably be happier if you occasionally watch movies or go sailing or talk to your children. That's because two hours on the golf course make a serious dent in the problem of "not playing enough golf"; now it's time to see what else in life is worthy of attention. Likewise, an investment in Microsoft makes a serious dent in the problem of adding some high-tech stocks to your portfolio; now it's time to move on to other investment goals.

But charity is different, because no matter how much you give to CARE, you will *never* make a serious dent in the problem of starving children. The problem is just too big; behind every starving child is another, equally deserving.

Giving to CARE is by no means a futile gesture; your contribution feeds a child, and feeding a child is equally worthwhile whether there are two or two hundred or two billion left unfed. When you're deciding whether to give to CARE in the first place, the right question is "How many children can I feed?" not "How many will I leave unfed?" So by all means give—to CARE, or to whoever else is first on your list. But the children left unfed—while quite irrelevant to your decision to give in the first place—move to center stage when you're deciding whether to move on to other good works.

At the university where I teach, a group of students has formed an organization to encourage charitable giving. Their mascot is Sammy the Starfish, and their literature explains why:

> A young girl was walking along a beach upon which thousands of starfish had been washed up during a terrible storm. When she came to each starfish, she would pick it up and throw it back into the ocean.
>
> She had been doing this for some time when a man approached her and said, "Little girl, why are you doing this? Look at this beach! You can't save all these starfish. You can't begin to make a difference!"
>
> The girl seemed crushed, suddenly deflated. But after a few moments, she bent down, picked up another starfish, and hurled it as far as she could into the ocean. Then she looked up at the man, and replied, "I made a difference to that one."

Score one for the little girl. Saving one starfish out of thousands is exactly as good as saving the only starfish on the beach.

If it's worth the trouble to save a starfish, then it's worth the trouble to save a starfish. You do what you can.

The story of Sammy has such a good moral, and conveys it so forcefully, that I've been moved to write a sequel:

> About an hour later, the man returned and asked the little girl whether she had noticed the pile of sand dollars blown up by the same storm, a little farther down the beach. The girl nodded sadly.
>
> "Well," the man said, "you've been saving starfish all afternoon. But nobody's saving the sand dollars. Shouldn't you move down the beach and throw back sand dollars for a while? Shouldn't they have a turn?"
>
> "But," said the little girl, "there are still so many starfish to save."

The little girl scores again. She can't be in two places at once. She's already made the sad but necessary choice that she'd rather save a starfish than a sand dollar, and nothing relevant has changed since she made that choice. She's saved a lot of starfish, and that was well worth the effort. But the basic problem—countless starfish and countless sand dollars—remains as it was. If the problem is unchanged, the solution should be unchanged as well.

Of course, a little girl who manages to clear the beach of starfish might very well move on to sand dollars; the same is true even of a little girl who has managed to save all the "worthiest" starfish, by whatever standards of worthiness she cares to apply—the healthiest, or the cutest, or the easiest to throw.

Once you've made a dent in a problem, it *can* be time to move on to the next.

So my "choose one and stick to it" argument doesn't apply to small charities. If your local theater group needs $100 for costumes and another $100 for a cast party, you might want to contribute the first $100 and not the second. You've made a dent in their problems and can justify moving on.

Likewise, if ten starving children show up at your door and you have ten hamburgers to give out, you won't want to give them all to the first child in line. One hamburger is enough to make a dent in that child's hunger problem; now it's time to turn your attention elsewhere. That's why it makes sense for mother birds to feed all their nestlings, not just the loudest.

But if ten *thousand* starving children show up at your door, where the first thousand are suffering from scurvy, the second thousand from rickets, the third thousand from something else, and so on, and if you feed a scurvy victim first, there's no reason to feed a rickets victim second. If the scurvy victims strike you as the neediest, you should keep feeding scurvy victims. Even if the rickets victims seem exactly as needy, there's no particular reason to switch.

Feeding one of ten thousand children is exactly as laudable as feeding one of ten or one who stands alone. But unlike feeding a single child, feeding one of ten thousand makes no significant change in the problem you're trying to solve, which leaves you with no reason to diversify.

Yet people constantly ignore my good advice by contributing to the American Heart Association, the American Cancer Society, CARE, and public radio all in the same afternoon—as if they were thinking, "OK, I've pretty much wrapped up the problem of heart disease; now let's see what I can do about cancer." But such delusions of grandeur must be rare. So there has to be some other reason why people diversify their charitable giving. What could that reason be?

Let me propose an answer. Some people give because they care about the recipients. Others give because they want to feel good about themselves. If you care about the recipients, you'll pick the worthiest and concentrate your efforts. But if you care about your own sense of satisfaction, you'll enjoy pointing to ten different charities and saying, "I gave to *all* of those!"

Your gift to CARE makes a dent in your own desire to contribute, but not in the problem CARE is trying to address. So if you're focusing on your own needs, you might be ready to move on to another charity, but if you're focusing on the children's needs, you won't be.

The impulse for self-satisfaction is by no means wicked, and when it leads to good works, it can be entirely laudable—but it's not the same thing as charity. To see the difference—and to see that diversification is a symptom of something other than a purely charitable impulse—try this thought experiment. Suppose you intend to give $100 to CARE. Now suppose that just before you mail your check, you learn that *I* have just contributed $100 to CARE. Do you then say, "In that case, I can skip my CARE contribution and go on to the Cancer Society?" I bet not.

But if *my* $100 contribution to CARE doesn't make you feel like you can go on to the Cancer Society, then why should *your* $100 contribution to CARE make you feel like you can go on to the Cancer Society? That can't make sense unless you believe that your $100 is either more effective or more important than my $100. If you think your giving is more effective than mine, you're suffering from a delusion of grandeur. If you think your giving is more important than mine, you've elevated your own desire for satisfaction over the recipients' need for food.

Some questions and some answers:

Question 1: What about risk aversion? Suppose I'm pretty sure that either one of Charity A and Charity B will use my money wisely, but I'm not sure which. Doesn't it make sense to split my contribution, to avoid the risk of putting all my eggs in the wrong basket?

Answer: It makes sense only if you believe that putting all your eggs in the wrong basket would be a great disaster. But that's another delusion of grandeur, because your contribution is a small fraction of the whole. It would indeed be disastrous if almost *everyone's* eggs were in the wrong basket, but splitting your personal contribution does essentially nothing to avert that disaster.

The eggs-in-the-basket analogy is seductive, and in some cases it's even accurate. It's correct, for example, to say that investing all your money in one stock is a big mistake because you might choose a bad stock. But it's incorrect to say that giving all your contributions to one charity is a big mistake because you might choose a bad charity. The difference is that you're the only contributor to your investment portfolio, but you are not the only contributor to your charity. So you're in danger of causing major damage to your portfolio, but not to your charity.

Question 2: But if everyone likes Charity A just slightly more than Charity B, and if everyone follows your advice, then Charity A ends up with all the money. Isn't that a disaster?

Answer: What makes you think Charity A ends up with all the money? In deciding where to contribute, you are perfectly free to account for other people's contributions. Once Charity A has collected enough to fulfill its primary goals, a lot of contributors will want to give Charity B a second look.

In other words, a charity's worthiness depends not just on what it's doing, but on how much it's already got. No individual can make a dent in Charity A's problem, but your neighbors can collectively make a dent, and once they do, you and others will want to move on to something else. So even when no individual diversifies, the community as a whole will diversify, as well it should.

Question 3: So does that mean I should give all my money to the charity with the smallest endowment?

Answer: Of course not. Endowments are only one of many relevant considerations. If I'm forced to choose between a cancer foundation with an endowment of $200 million and a foundation to build luxury homes for earthworms with an endowment of $10, I'll go with the cancer foundation.

With very few exceptions, the logic of pure charity precludes diversifying. But the few exceptions are worth noting.

First, there's the "small charity" exception that I've already discussed in the context of local theater groups. If my neighbor is starving, I'll buy him a meal; now that he's merely hungry, I might let him fend for himself.

Second, there's an exception for donations of time, as opposed to money. That's because tasks tend to become more tedious when you've been at them awhile. After two hours of standing on your feet in the soup kitchen, you might prefer to donate your third hour to a charity you can serve while sitting down.

Third, there's an exception when new information becomes available. If you learn something new and positive about the Cancer Society, you might want to switch your targeting to the Cancer Society and away from CARE. But that exception does not apply to people who mail checks to three different charities in a single five-minute interval.

Fourth, there might be an exception for situations where you believe your own contributions can inspire others to give. Then you might prefer to spread your beneficence widely, to make it more visible and more likely to trigger the charitable impulses of your neighbors. As one of my readers pointed out, "If I give $50 each to NPR, Amnesty International, and the ACLU, I can mention this to my friends when discussions of public radio, human rights, or civil rights arise."

But taken to its logical extreme, this argument suggests that instead of giving $100 to CARE, you should give a penny apiece to each of 10,000 different charities. Does that strategy inspire emulation? On the contrary, it sends a message that you're not serious about any of these causes, and destroys whatever value you might have as a role model.

The same dynamic is at work whenever you diversify. Give $100 to CARE and you send your neighbors the message that CARE is a worthy cause. Give $100 to the Cancer Society and you send the message that maybe CARE wasn't so worthy after all.

So diversifying to inspire others could be counterproductive. Besides, if you really believe that others are so readily influenced by your behavior, you can always *tell* them you've given far more than you actually have. (On the other hand, most of us have an aversion to lying.)

Finally, you might want to diversify if someone rewards you for it—your employer, for example. Maybe your employer has a matching program that kicks in more when you diversify. But this observation replaces one mystery with another. It explains why you diversify, but fails to explain why your employer wants you to. Presumably, your employer is motivated by something other than a purely charitable impulse. Chances are you don't find that discovery terribly surprising.

Indeed, American corporations are essentially immune to charitable impulses. This is for the good and sufficient reason that stockholders don't want corporate executives to choose their charities for them. You hire a tailor to make your clothes, you hire a carpenter to fix your roof, and, if you're a stockholder, you hire executives to run your company. Your tailor, your carpenter, and your executives might be very good at what they do, but it doesn't follow that they'd also be good at figuring out how to give away your money.

So for the most part, corporations eschew charity completely. Instead, they truckle to the public-relations circus known as the United Way.

Nothing could be less charitable than giving to the United Way. Among the several dozen agencies that receive United Way handouts, surely you can identify—with essentially zero effort— at least one that, according to your own beliefs and values, will make better than average use of an extra dollar. (If you *can't* identify such an agency, you might win the world record for obliviousness to the needs of others.) Allowing the United Way to split your contribution among thousands of less-worthy causes is the very opposite of charity. Your employer's public-relations department might love you for it, but you purchase that esteem by diverting resources away from the worthiest recipients, a complete perversion of what charity is supposed to be about.

Social scientists distinguish between *de*scriptive theories, which describe how people *do* behave, and *pre*scriptive theories, which describe how people *should* behave. Economists are traditionally humble enough to restrict themselves to pure description.

So here is the purely descriptive version of this chapter: charitable people would not diversify their contributions; most people *do* diversify their contributions; therefore, most people are motivated by something other than charity.

Traditional economics tells me to stop there. We've learned something about human nature, and that's a sufficient accomplishment. Our job is to understand people, not to change them.

But in this case, I am inclined to deviate from the party line and offer a *pre*scriptive version of the theory. Something like this: if you are trying to be charitable, then you *ought* to target a single charity instead of diversifying your contributions.

Why is this theory different from all other theories? Partly because the argument runs so counter to intuition that I suspect most people have never considered it. So I find it plausible that once the argument has been presented, some people will want to rethink their behavior.

I am one of those people. When I first heard this argument—

in a conversation over lunch—I instinctively recoiled from it, which is another way of saying that I failed to understand it. I raised a dozen false objections, and it took me a long time to see why they were false. Even after I'd grasped the logic, it took me a while longer to incorporate it into my natural thought processes. Only then did I adjust my giving habits. So I make bold to offer a prescriptive theory, driven as I am by the ardor of a convert.

Giving for the purpose of self-congratulation is still giving, and it is surely to be welcomed, but it would be charitable to call it charity. We have been told on reasonably high authority that true charity vaunteth not itself; it is not puffed up. You can puff yourself up with thank-you notes from a dozen organizations, or you can be truly charitable by concentrating your efforts where you believe they will do the most good.

Addendum: A Defense of Pure Reason

When I published an abbreviated version of this chapter in *Slate*, I got a flood of email responses. Of course, some readers are more thoughtful than others, but I appreciate hearing from almost all of them. The disheartening exceptions are those who are hostile to the very *prospect* of thought.

Take, for example, the reader who dismissed this entire issue by asking: "Am I not allowed to believe that CARE and the American Cancer Society are both worthy charities, both deserving of my money?" Well, of course you are allowed to believe that; I believe it too, and so do most of the people I'd want to have as friends. But the question is: given your belief that both charities are worthy, do you not have some obligation, or at least some desire, to *think* about how best to translate that belief into action?

You can legitimately avoid confronting that dilemma only if

you are one of those exceedingly rare individuals who can think of only one charity worthy of your consideration. The rest of us—my correspondent included—must somehow reconcile our own conflicting values. (And yes, starving children and cancer research are surely conflicting values, because every dollar you give to one is a dollar you didn't give to the other.) When your own values conflict with one another, there are only two ways to go. You can operate on blind instinct, or you can try using a little logic to figure out what those values require of you. I advocate the latter course.

Often the best way to make sure you're being logical is to express your arguments mathematically. Early in this century, the eminent economist Alfred Marshall offered this advice to his colleagues: when confronted with an economic problem, first translate into mathematics, then solve the problem, then translate back into English and burn the mathematics. I am a devotee of Marshall and frequently follow his advice. But some readers will want to see the mathematics so they can judge for themselves what's been lost in translation; for their benefit, I've put the math in the appendix to this book.

Resistance to logic frequently reveals itself as animosity toward mathematics. Some of my *Slate* readers even maintained that no mathematically expressible argument can ever be relevant to a moral dilemma. But "mathematically expressible" is the same thing as "internally consistent," so apparently these readers believe that it's not possible to contribute to moral discourse unless you intentionally contradict yourself.

That's not to say that you should let yourself be swayed by mathematical mumbo jumbo, or even by legitimate mathematics that you happen not to understand. If the mathematics failed to capture the meaning of the argument, or if the argument itself were flawed, the mathematics would add nothing. But in this case, there's nothing in the mathematics that isn't also in the English. The mathematics is there only to keep us honest, and to guard against subtle inconsistencies.

It's important to distinguish what a mathematician would call "first-order benefits" (like saving a starving child) from "second-order benefits" (like substantially reducing the number of starving children in the world). First-order benefits justify charitable giving, but it takes second-order benefits to justify charitable diversification. Calculus happens to be a particularly convenient language for keeping track of those subtleties. Why would anyone object to introducing precise language into a difficult moral argument that demands precision?

Moral issues are worthy of serious attention. That's why moral discourse cannot afford to exclude the great power of mathematics to identify the essential and strip away the irrelevant. When (as I've done in the appendix) you can take all the things you care about, collectively name them F, and establish a surprising and important truth that does not depend on what F is—so that your discovery applies equally well to you and to your brother-in-law, with whom you never agree on anything—then you have learned something profound. When we're sorting out our moral obligations, profundity is worth striving for.

THIRTEEN
THE CENTRAL BANKER
OF THE SOUL

It has always seemed to me that the two great mysteries of the Universe are "Why is there something instead of nothing?" and "Why do people lock their refrigerator doors?" Long ago, I reached the reluctant conclusion that there was nothing intelligible to be said on either subject. Now, thanks to some remarkable new ideas in physics, philosophy, and economics, I've begun to think otherwise.

We need new ideas because there are no old ideas; there are only timeworn dismissals that invoke God's will and the difficulty of dieting. Why, after all, would any rational creature want to erect an obstacle between itself and a midnight snack? Midnight snacks have both costs and benefits. The costs are usually measured in calories, or grams of fat, and as for the benefits— well, snacks must have benefits; otherwise they wouldn't tempt us. We snack when we believe the benefits exceed the costs; in other words, we snack when we believe that snacking is, on balance and in our best judgment, a good thing. What could be the point of making a good thing more difficult?

But people do lock their refrigerators. They also hide cigarettes from themselves, invest their savings in accounts designed to discourage withdrawals, and adopt comically elaborate schemes to force themselves to exercise. Odysseus resisted the Sirens' call by lashing himself to the mast. I used to lock my computer in a drawer every afternoon and then order my secretary to hide the key so I couldn't spend all day surfing the Net.

None of which seems to make any sense. If I'm willing to sacrifice an afternoon's work to Net-surfing, Net-surfing must be worth the sacrifice—so why should I stop myself from Net-surfing? I eat hot fudge sundaes when I want them enough to justify the calories. If I want them enough to justify the calories, why should I stop myself from eating them?

Here's the cheap response: "The sundae *isn't* worth the calories (or the cigarette isn't worth the health risk, or the frolic with the Sirens isn't worth the shipwreck), but I know that in the heat of the moment I'll become irrational and make the wrong decision." My friend David Friedman—one of the sharpest and most tenacious economic thinkers I've ever known—buys that answer. David teaches at Santa Clara University, where he refuses to accept a parking permit because he wants to force himself to bicycle to work. When he was accused of irrationality (after all, rational creatures know they're going to bike at all the right times anyway, so why not take a parking permit to use on a rainy day?), David cheerfully concurred. He explained that there are two kinds of human behavior: rational and irrational. When it comes to predicting other people's behavior (in other words, when he's doing economics), he focuses exclusively on the rational part, because the irrational part is inherently unpredictable. But when it comes to predicting his *own* behavior, he thinks he has some special insight into his personal brand of irrationality, so he can acknowledge it and plan around it.

In other words, David—possibly for the only time in his intellectual career—gave up without a fight. When it comes to explaining human behavior, "irrationality" should be a desperate last resort—not because people are never irrational, but because the attempt to find rational explanations is enlightening. If someone does something you don't understand, you can either dismiss it as irrational or try to figure out its purpose. The former course offers an opportunity to feel smugly superior; the latter offers a chance to learn something.

So unlike David, I want to start from the presumption that when people eat sundaes, smoke cigarettes, and drive instead of biking, they're rationally (though not necessarily consciously) weighing costs against benefits and making the best choices they can. The riddle is: how can it be rational to try to restrain yourself from making rational choices?

The easiest—and silliest—solution is to posit a "taste" for self-control. If people just happen to enjoy locking their refrigerators even more than they enjoy eating hot fudge sundaes, then it's rational to indulge that taste by locking the refrigerator. But once you allow yourself to posit "tastes" for everything under the sun, you abandon all intellectual discipline—any behavior at all can be "explained" by the assertion that somebody had a taste for it. My first economics teacher, Deirdre McCloskey, used to warn against hollow triumphs like "Why did the man drink the motor oil? Because he had a *taste* for drinking motor oil!" If you can explain anything, you've explained nothing.

But in his entirely marvelous book on *How the Mind Works*, cognitive scientist Steven Pinker suggests that we can safely posit a taste for self-control without opening the floodgates that would allow us to posit a taste for drinking motor oil. Here's why:

unlike a taste for drinking motor oil, a taste for self-control confers a reproductive advantage.

When you snack at midnight, you get most of the benefits, but your spouse (who has good reasons to care about your health and appearance) shares many of the costs. So a taste for self-restraint makes you more desirable in the marriage market. Therefore, we shouldn't be surprised that natural selection favored people with a taste for locking their own refrigerators.

In other words, a locked refrigerator is a babe magnet. Dieting alone won't do, because no matter how trim you are, the babes are smart enough to suspect you'll revert to your natural gluttony if they're unwise enough to marry you. You could try to finesse this problem with a prenuptial agreement that limits you to two desserts a day, but enforcement would be a nightmare. But if the babes can see that you actually have a *taste* for self-control, they might be sufficiently reassured to take a chance on you.

Likewise with cigarettes. Say you've weighed the pleasures of smoking against the risks of lung disease and decided it makes sense for you to smoke. That's going to make it a little harder to attract a partner willing to stand by you in sickness and in health. So you'll do better on the marriage market if you have a visible instinct to restrain yourself from smoking *even though, for you, smoking is the right choice.*

And likewise with David Friedman and his refusal to accept a parking permit. For some people—and perhaps for David—it's rational to drive to work every day, even at the cost of some physical unfitness. But that physical unfitness would make David's wife Betty unhappy. So my theory is that David gives up his parking permit to reassure Betty that, perhaps contrary to his own narrowly defined interests, he'll keep biking. That makes David a more desirable husband, so Betty works a little harder to keep him happy.

Now you might object that not everybody is looking for a mate. But everybody has *ancestors* who, at one time or another, looked (and looked successfully!) for a mate. A taste that helped your ancestors reproduce is likely to be passed on. From that point of view, a taste for self-control is no more mysterious than a taste for sex.

In the classic American game of "chicken," two cretins drive cars straight at each other until one of them loses by swerving. The key to success in this game is convincing your opponent that no matter what happens, you will never swerve. Therefore the winning strategy is to rip out your steering column and make sure your opponent sees you do it.* The moral is that freedom isn't always a good thing. The freedom to swerve is the freedom to lose. Throw away that freedom and you're more likely to win.

If you've ever applied for a mortgage, you've thrown away some freedom by agreeing to make monthly payments and solemnizing that agreement with a contract. The sacrifice is justified because without it, your loan would never be approved. In fact, it's not enough to sign the contract; your loan won't be approved unless your banker believes you intend to take the contract seriously. The key to success is convincing the banker that no matter what happens, you will never default. Therefore, the winning strategy is to promise credibly that you'll commit hara-kiri if you ever miss a payment. But words are not enough. A credible promise requires a credible enforcer. If the government wants to provide meaningful assistance to first-time home buy-

---

* Your opponent's best counterstrategy is to refuse to look at you, in which case you might as well leave your steering column intact.

ers, it should probably consider capital punishment for late mortgage payments.

Governments have their own credibility problems. For example, national governments like to promise investors that the money supply will grow stably and predictably; such a promise encourages investment and fosters economic growth. Unfortunately, governments are perpetually tempted to break the promise by manipulating the money supply in pursuit of short-term goals. Investors are smart enough to foresee that temptation and hence to doubt the promise. To address this problem, most Western governments have intentionally curtailed their own freedom to control the money supply, by appointing independent central bankers who are not directly answerable to the government.*

Appointing a central banker, like signing a mortgage contract or ripping out your steering column, is a conscious policy, deliberately designed to limit your own freedom in order to make your promises more credible. By contrast, a taste for locking refrigerators or hiding cigarettes is an unconscious drive, the product not of design but of random mutations winnowed by natural selection. Therefore its purpose is hidden from us; locking the refrigerator doesn't *feel* like a mating strategy. But that's nothing out of the ordinary. After all, our zest for fresh fruits and sizzling steaks doesn't *feel* like a strategy for gathering basic nutrients; nevertheless, it evolved because there was a time when those who liked food were those who survived. The joy of recreational sex doesn't *feel* like part of a drive to reproduce; nevertheless, it evolved because there was a time when those who liked sex were those who had offspring.

In principle, Nature could have followed a very different

---

* In the United States, the central bank is called the Federal Reserve, and (as of this writing) the central banker is Ben Bernanke.

course. Instead of making food and sex enjoyable, it could have endowed us with enough brainpower to recognize that food and sex are necessary for survival and reproduction. Instead of thinking "Boy, that steak looks good," you'd think "I'm a little low on amino acids; time to eat some steak." Instead of thinking "Boy, that new neighbor looks good," you'd think "That new neighbor has some traits that would be useful to my offspring; time to swap some DNA." In a lot of ways, that would have been more efficient—we wouldn't eat foods that are bad for us, and we wouldn't waste time and energy pursuing nonprocreative sex. Offsetting those advantages would be the need for a brain capable of calculating when it's time to eat. For one reason or another, we evolved more in the direction of unconscious instincts. So instead of saying "I'll lock the refrigerator because it improves my prospects in the marriage market," you just feel a strange compulsion to lock the refrigerator.

In fact, unlike eating and copulating, locking the refrigerator *has* to be an unconscious instinct in order to work. If it were part of a conscious mating strategy, you'd predictably abandon it as soon as you'd found a mate. Only by removing the behavior from your conscious control can you reassure potential mates that it will continue past the wedding ceremony.

Making commitments is both easy and meaningless; making *enforceable* commitments is both difficult and purposeful. So humans, by intent, and nature, by natural selection, devote considerable effort to concocting enforcement mechanisms. Humans invent central banks; Nature invents instincts. Instincts are good enforcement mechanisms because we are so clearly at their mercy.

Take, for example, the instinct for revenge. Revenge has been called the one debt that is always paid promptly and with pleasure. Ironically, it's also the one debt that's entirely voluntary. Disregard your mortgage and you'll hear from the bank; disregard an insult and nobody comes around to collect.

Repaying voluntary debt can be a costly extravagance. The great dynasties of Lancaster and York were annihilated in the whirlwind of vengeance that swept England in the late fifteenth century; four centuries later, a succession of Hatfields and McCoys died for the privilege of killing their rivals in a legendary Appalachian feud. Why couldn't they all just get along?

Francis Bacon, a servant of the Tudor dynasty that arose from the ashes of Lancaster and York, explained why it's best to let bygones be bygones:

> That which is past is gone and irrevocable, and wise men have enough to do with things present and to come. . . . a man that studieth revenge keeps his own wounds green, which otherwise would heal and do well.

As a writer, I note with considerable dismay that although Bacon's advice is clear, succinct, profound, and apparently irrefutable, it has been in print for over three hundred years without any discernible effect on human behavior.

How could an instinct that is invariably self-destructive have survived the vagaries of natural selection? Political scientists have long recognized that while revenge itself is costly and pointless, the *threat* of revenge is an effective deterrent. Unfortunately, coming from a cold-bloodedly rational creature, the threat is an empty one. It becomes credible only when it is driven by pure instinct—in other words, if you want to scare off your enemies, you need a *taste* for revenge.

In a passage so fascinating that I wish I could plagiarize it in its entirety, Steven Pinker observes that we signal our anger largely through muscle contractions that cannot be triggered voluntarily—thereby informing our neighbors that our emotions are genuine, and that our power to override them is limited. Just as the government enhances its credibility by ceding control to the central bank, we gain credibility by ceding control to our emotions. A passion for revenge is the central banker of the soul.

Economists have a name for all this; we call it the *time-inconsistency* problem—the difficulty of committing yourself to a course of action that everyone knows you'll want to abandon in the future. The only reason to make such commitments is that they influence your relationships with other people. If you never interact with anyone, you'll never have a problem with time inconsistency. Time inconsistency is born of conflict.

The people we interact with most intimately are undoubtedly our own future selves. The key feature of that interaction is a high degree of altruism; we make current sacrifices for future rewards. But what kind of altruism do we practice? Is it an altruism so pure that conflict is impossible? Or is it an imperfect altruism that invites time inconsistency?

When my friend Ralph Cohen announced that his wife was pregnant, I asked what path he hoped his child would follow. "It doesn't matter," said Ralph. "If he's happy, I'll be happy." Then, after a thoughtful pause, he added, "My personal preference is shortstop. But anything he wants to do is fine with me." Then, after a longer pause: "As long as it's in the infield."

That's the difference between pure altruism, where you care about other people's happiness (though perhaps not as urgently as you care about your own) and what I've called "imperfect altruism," where you reserve the right to care about how others *achieve* their happiness.

When it comes to our own future selves, traditional economic theory insists that we're pure altruists—we want to be happy in the future, though perhaps not as urgently as we want to be happy in the present. Harvard professor David Laibson is one of a few iconoclasts who disagree. Nobody doubts that we are imperfectly altruistic toward others; Laibson argues that we can also be imperfectly altruistic toward ourselves—by caring not just about our own future happiness, but about how that happiness is achieved. And just as imperfect altruism toward your children can cause conflict in your family, imperfect altruism toward your future self can cause conflict in your soul.

For example: Everyone knows that a taste for expensive pleasures can ruin your life. But if you're an imperfect altruist, then a taste for *anticipating* expensive pleasures can ruin your life in a far more interesting way. If your greatest joy in life is looking forward to tomorrow's extravagance, you've got a problem: tomorrow is a moving target. On Monday, you plan a lavish party for Tuesday; when Tuesday arrives, you indulge your preference for anticipation by postponing the party till Wednesday. The postponements continue until you die and leave a large estate.

The tragedy here is not that you never get to spend your money; the tragedy is that you never even get to *anticipate* spending your money, because you're smart enough to foresee the whole sequence of events before it even unfolds. If you love looking forward to parties, and if you know you love looking forward to parties, then you can never look forward to a party. (Maybe this was what Bertolt Brecht meant when he said his life had been ruined by intelligence.) The solution, if you can manage it, is to plan a party that can't be postponed. Pay the caterer well in advance, and be sure to choose one who will penalize you heavily for a last-minute cancellation.

I suffer from a minor but aggravating form of this affliction: I avoid reading really good books, because it robs me of the pleasure of looking forward to them. Of course, knowing this about myself, I never get to look forward to them either. Air travel has been my salvation: I force myself to read good books by trapping myself with them on airplanes. If they ever upgrade those in-flight magazines into a plausible reading alternative, I'll be ruined.

My friend Ray Heitmann suffers from the opposite problem: instead of looking forward to extravagance, he likes to anticipate his own future frugality. He particularly enjoys believing that after a certain age, he won't spend resources to prolong his own life. But he's painfully aware that the "certain age" keeps getting redefined so it's always safely in the future. Therefore, he's looking for ways to limit his own future freedom of choice.

If Ray cared only about his own future happiness (that is, if Ray were perfectly altruistic toward his future self), then you could fairly accuse him of inconsistency: limiting your choices can't make you happier. But Ray cares also about how he *achieves* his future happiness, which makes him an imperfect altruist, but a consistent one. If your altruism is imperfect, you can want your future self to throw a party (or to read a book or to forgo expensive medical care, or for that matter, to save money or to quit smoking), even though you know your future self would prefer otherwise.

When Dorothy Parker lamented that "I hate writing, but I love having written," she was expressing the sort of routine trade-off between current costs and future benefits that fits right into a traditional economic framework. Laibson's imperfect altruists face a far subtler problem—they're not just weighing costs and benefits, they're engaged in games of strategy against their future selves.

That suggests a new and different answer to my question about refrigerator locks. I've spent most of this chapter arguing that the lock resolves a conflict between you (who believe that a hot fudge sundae is worth the calories) and your mate, or potential mate (who believes otherwise). According to Laibson, the conflict is not between you and your mate, but between you-today and you-tomorrow.

Whichever theory is right, there's one thing we can be sure of: the door locks remain inexplicable unless you are in conflict with *someone*. If all you want for your future self is happiness, and if there's no third party involved, there can be no good reason to restrict your future options.

How plausible is Laibson's theory? We won't know till we've explored its implications. Professors Per Krusell and Anthony Smith have begun that process by asking themselves what kind of savings behavior we would observe in a world full of Laibsonites. Orthodox economic theory predicts that if two people have identical preferences and identical opportunities, then they'll adopt identical savings habits. Krusell and Smith point out that in a world of Laibson-style preferences, nothing of the sort is true.

Here's why: Imagine two imperfect altruists, Albert and Alvin, who want their future selves to be not just happy, but also frugal. Albert's a pessimist who expects his future self to be a spendthrift; Alvin's an optimist who expects to practice lifelong self-control. Albert doesn't want his money squandered by the wastrel he expects to become, so he figures he might as well spend it all today. Alvin, on the other hand, faces the heartening prospect of passing his savings on into the good hands of his own future self, and is thereby encouraged to save.

Both Albert's and Alvin's behaviors are self-reinforcing from one year to the next. They have the same preferences and the same opportunities, but one dies poor and the other dies rich.

Other implications are even more bizarre. Alice is an imperfect altruist who enjoys contemplating her own future extravagance (as opposed to Albert and Alvin, who hope to be frugal). Alice is initially optimistic that she *will* be extravagant, and therefore saves all her money to finance big parties in the future. But as soon as she realizes she's become a "saver," she loses confidence in her future extravagance and figures she might as well spend her money today—whereupon she realizes she's a "spender" and goes back to saving. Her expectations—and the behavior that stems from them—fluctuate wildly forever.

Exploring implications is one way to test Laibson's theory. Another is to ask whether Laibson-style preferences are plausible in the first place. Is the assumption of imperfect altruism too glib and easy, like the assumption of a taste for motor oil? Or can it be justified by an appeal to natural selection, like a taste for revenge?

Here's a wild speculation: maybe Laibson-style preferences lead to visible attempts at self-control, and visible attempts at self-control are reassuring to potential mates, hence are favored by natural selection. If that speculation stands up to some reasonable tests (say, a computer simulation of resource competition among individuals with evolving preferences), it could tie the two refrigerator-lock theories together into a single neat package.

Now as to the origin of the Universe—or, as I prefer to phrase the question, "Where did all this stuff come from?"—here is what I believe: The Universe is a pure mathematical pattern—not a pattern *in* anything, but the pattern itself. Patterns don't need to come from anywhere; they just are. The particular pattern that constitutes the Universe happens to contain subpatterns that are sufficiently complex in just the right way to be aware of their own existence. That's us.

To me, this rings absolutely true, though half my friends think it's clearly wrong and the other half can't figure out what I'm talking about.

But there might be a good economic reason for that. Steven Pinker points out that understanding the origin of the Universe is not a terribly useful skill; it confers no reproductive advantage, so there's no reason we should have evolved brains capable of thinking about such a question. Nature is too good an economist to invest in such frivolities. On the other hand, the ability to understand human behavior has clear payoffs for a social animal like *Homo sapiens.* So it's not too much to hope that we could work out a detailed and convincing theory of refrigerator locks.

FOURTEEN
HOW TO READ THE NEWS

The problem with the news is that it tends to be reported by journalism majors. That's probably better than letting them design bridges, but it does call for a certain skepticism on the part of the reader.

Even when the facts are right, the interpretation can be very wrong—especially on hot-button issues like racial profiling or outsourcing, where prejudices run deep. If you want to know what's really happening, a little economic analysis can go a long way. Some examples:

Racial Profiling
If you were driving along the Maryland stretch of I-95 a few years back, you might have been stopped for a drug search. Especially

if you were black. Blacks were three-and-a-half times as likely as whites to be stopped and searched.

How come? Theory One is that the police concentrated on blacks because blacks were more prone to carry drugs. Theory Two is that the police didn't like black people.

Let's look at the evidence. Among whites who were stopped, about one-third of one percent were caught with drugs. Among blacks who were stopped, the fraction was—almost exactly the same. Aha! So blacks and whites are equally prone to carry drugs. The police must be racists. No?

Think again. Remember that blacks carried drugs just as frequently as whites *even though they were three-and-a-half times as likely to be stopped.* Imagine how many more drugs they'd have carried if they'd been treated equally!

The correct conclusion is that in that time and in that place and for whatever reason, blacks had a much greater propensity than whites to carry drugs—a propensity tempered only by the scrutiny of law enforcement. (Of course, this argument makes sense only if blacks are *aware* that they're being stopped more frequently than whites—but given the ubiquity of complaints about racial profiling, this seems like a natural assumption.) Another correct conclusion is that the police had no particular animus toward black people.

Here's why: Think about what happens if the police single-mindedly attempt to maximize the number of drug convictions. They start by focusing their attention on the group with the higher propensity to carry drugs—in this case blacks. That makes it easier for white drug carriers to slip through the net, and harder for black drug carriers. Because people respond to incentives, the number of white drug carriers grows and the number of black drug carriers shrinks.

That continues until whites and blacks are carrying drugs in equal proportions. At that point (which could have been reached long before data started being collected in 1994), there's no reason to crack down on blacks any further, but no reason to ease up on them either. (And any temporary easing would quickly lead to a discrepancy between black and white conviction rates and a return to the equilibrium.)

If the police actually bore some animus toward blacks, you'd expect them to go further—cracking down on blacks to the point where very few blacks would dare to carry drugs. Then we'd see a lower conviction rate for blacks than for whites. Instead we see *equal* conviction rates, which suggests that the police concentrate on stopping blacks right up to the point where it helps them increase their conviction rates, but no further.*

By that standard, it's not blacks but Hispanics who have cause for complaint. Stopped Hispanics are only about a third as likely to be carrying drugs as stopped whites or stopped blacks. Why would the police stop a Hispanic who has a one-ninth of one percent chance of carrying drugs instead of a black or white who has a one-third of one percent chance of carrying drugs? Arguably, it's because they have something against Hispanics.

Hispanics aside, the evidence strongly favors the hypothesis that the police are looking to arrest and convict as many drug dealers as possible, regardless of race. That's good, right? No, it's bad. Exactly *why* it's bad depends on how you feel about the Drug War.

If, like me, you consider the Drug War a moral outrage, you'll be distressed to learn that the police are maximizing drug convictions. Stopping motorists because you don't like their race is reprehensible, but at least it doesn't retard economic activity. If the police are going to harass a dozen motorists a day, it

* See the appendix for discussion of some subtleties in this argument.

doesn't much matter whether they target blacks, whites, or a representative sample; twelve harassed motorists are twelve harassed motorists. But it *does* matter whether they target drug dealers, because that discourages the drug trade and raises the price of drugs. That strikes me as bad—and in fact, worse than racism.

Of course, if, unlike me, you're a committed Drug Warrior, you'll consider discouraging the drug trade a good thing. So you might think a committed Drug Warrior would applaud a police policy of maximizing drug convictions. Think again. If you really want to retard drug traffic, you should maximize not convictions, but deterrence. And to maximize deterrence, you should probably stop more whites, because there are more whites in the population to deter.

Searching mostly blacks can be simultaneously a very good way to make lots of drug arrests and a very poor way to slow down drug traffic. That's because it advertises to whites that they have little to fear from the police, which emboldens more whites to carry drugs. And because there are so many white people around, this effect can be quite large. After all, one-third of one percent of whites represents a lot more motorists—and a lot more drugs—than one-third of one percent of blacks.

So whether you're for or against the Drug War, you've got a good reason to emulate the ACLU and call for a more racially balanced stop-and-search policy. There would be fewer arrests (to appeal to the libertarians) and greater deterrence (to appeal to the prohibitionists).

When the Maryland statistics first hit the news, virtually every commentator misread their significance. Some saw evidence of racism, some saw evidence of effective drug enforcement, and all of them were wrong. Racist police would have stopped even more blacks; police who cared about deterrence (as opposed to convictions) would have stopped more whites. A little economic reasoning would have served everyone well.

Disaster Relief

It takes a callous soul indeed to look at television images of disaster victims and wish government assistance on them. Especially when the victims are poor.

After Hurricane Katrina devastated New Orleans, the federal government rushed in with $200 billion to rebuild and aid the victims. With that single thoughtless act, the government made life harder for poor people all over the country who are doing their best to scrape by.

Here's why: Poor people, far more than rich people, need to watch their budgets. They buy cheaper clothes, cheaper food, and cheaper housing. They're even willing to live on floodplains and risk occasional devastation if the housing is cheap enough. That's why, in New Orleans, it was poor people who were disproportionately hit by Katrina—they were the ones who lived below sea level.

Each city, and each neighborhood within each city, offers its own package of amenities, risk, and housing prices. So people have choices. They can live cheaply but dangerously, or they can pay more and be safer. (Of course, risk is only one of the things that affect housing prices. Even though it's built on a fault line, San Francisco, thanks to its spectacular amenities, is a very expensive place to live—but still a lot cheaper than it would be without the earthquakes. And the most quake-prone areas of the city are the least expensive.)

But a policy of federal disaster assistance tends to erase that choice by forcing everyone to share the flood risk—and consequently bringing housing prices closer together. If the government stands ready to (literally) bail out New Orleans by raising taxes in Kansas City, then New Orleans housing prices rise and Kansas City housing prices fall. You can no longer escape the risk of a flood by moving to Kansas City; you can no longer reap the benefits of accepting the full risk by moving to New Orleans.

That's no clear improvement for anyone. Those who preferred to accept some risk are now forced to live more expensively; those who preferred to live safely and pay for it are now forced to participate (through the tax system) in the risk taking of others. That kind of homogenization, ironically, is exactly what the city of New Orleans has always stood against. It's good to have cities with different cultures, it's good to have cities with different musical heritages, and it's good to have cities with different risk characteristics. Without differences, how can we celebrate diversity?

Because poor people disproportionately choose cheap housing, poor people are disproportionately hurt when disaster-assistance policies make cheap housing more expensive. If your concern is that poor people shouldn't be so poor in the first place, my response is that you don't have to wait for a flood to raise that issue. The specific flood-related policy question is this: *given* the population of poor people, do we make them better or worse off when we give them disaster relief (which is good) and simultaneously raise their housing costs (which is bad)? The refusal to engage that question is, it seems to me, nothing short of a declaration of indifference to what actually benefits the poor.

You might say that what we really owe the poor is disaster assistance *and* affordable housing. You might as well say that we owe them all magical pink unicorns that produce an unlimited supply of milk. It is quite simply impossible to guarantee assistance to people living on a floodplain without affecting their housing costs. And it is quite simply unserious to declare your commitment to poor people without pausing to ask whether a pet program does poor people more harm than good.

The Sack of Baghdad

In 2003, as Baghdad plunged into chaos, looters ransacked the National Museum, escaping with hundreds of clay pots, figurines, stone tablets, and a whole lot of other useless junk. Oh, yes, and a 2,600-year-old harp, which I guarantee you makes far less beautiful music than what I can get for free off the World Wide Web. I mention this because I wrote a column in *Slate* that minimized the importance of looters making off with jars of peanut butter, and was deluged with email asking "But what about the museum?" Well, what about it? A lot of stuff in that museum was five thousand years old. If it were in my garage, I'd have swept it out to the curb a long time ago.

Within twenty-four hours, it seemed like every editorial page in the Western world had drawn some analogy with the burning of the ancient Library of Alexandria. Give me a break. The Library of Alexandria was a repository of (among other things) useful knowledge, and a place where knowledge itself was advanced. Archimedes and Hero invented the science of hydraulics at Alexandria; Eratosthenes measured the circumference of the earth. The most advanced medicine, astronomy, and mathematics of the ancient world came from Alexandria. What earthshaking discovery ever emerged from the National Museum of Baghdad? Modern science and technology flow from Princeton, Paris, and Moscow, not from the ancient cradle of civilization.

If the Museum's holdings are not an important source of scientific learning, what *is* their value? Have we lost some great art? Well, I'm sure most of these artworks were great for their time—around 3000 BC or so—but artistic techniques have rather advanced since then. And I'm also sure there were some items in that museum which, if they had survived, would have shocked and awed future visitors with their splendor—a splendor which now can never be seen. But that's not a tragedy at the level of Alexandria; at worst it's a tragedy at the level of Dylan Thomas's death at age 39, before he could complete his masterpiece "In Country Heaven." In other words, it's the sort of tragedy that happens several times a decade, not the sort that happens once every couple of millennia. If it were up to me, I'd far prefer to have Dylan Thomas back to write another twenty years' worth of poetry than to spend an afternoon looking at even the greatest art that ancient Babylonia had to offer.

Besides, surely there are *pictures* of the *really* good stuff. The pictures might not be as good as the originals, but they're all that 99.9 percent of the world was ever going to see anyway. That's another difference between Alexandria and Baghdad: Much of the knowledge stored at Alexandria was lost along with the original manuscripts. Much of the knowledge stored at Baghdad—or anywhere else in the modern world—is stored in images that are retrievable at the click of a mouse.

What about history? Are there things it will now be impossible to know about the birth of civilization? Probably. And so what? I happen to like history a lot, but there's a lot of history to learn. If the looting means there will be one less book to read about ancient Sumer, I'll read one more book about medieval England instead, and I won't feel substantially impoverished by the substitution. If I—who am more of a history buff than 95 percent of the world's population—don't much mind seeing

Babylonian artifacts disappear, then why should anyone else care?

Knowledge of the past is extremely valuable. It does not follow that each additional *bit* of knowledge of the past is extremely valuable. In that sense, antiquities are a lot like water. Water in the aggregate is priceless; we couldn't live without it. But that doesn't mean we have to cry every time someone spills a bucket of water: We've got plenty of water to go around. Likewise, antiquities in the aggregate enrich our lives in many ways, but that doesn't mean we have to cry every time someone loots a museum. There are enough antiquities around to fulfill a lifetime of curiosity.

Put it this way: if you think your life is substantially poorer because of what's been lost in Baghdad, then you need a better life. There are more fascinating things in heaven and earth than you'll ever have time to contemplate. When one disappears, you replace it with another.

The great fallacy is believing that because artifacts are either expensive or irreplaceable, they have great social value. That's wrong for multiple reasons. First, many of those items were expensive only because of competition for them by museum curators spending other people's money. What other market is there for a 5,000-year-old slab?

Second, and much more important, there's never much reason to think that an artwork's social value is well reflected by its price. That's because works of art deflect attention from each other. Dan Brown wrote a book called *The Da Vinci Code* that sold over seven-and-a-half million copies and earned its author over $20 million, but that doesn't mean the world would be $20 million poorer without it. If *The Da Vinci Code* hadn't been written, some other now-unnoticed book might have taken its place as the blockbuster of the year, and readers would have been almost as happy.

A book is not an orange. If you grow the best orange in the world, the second-best orange still gets eaten. But if you write the best book in the world, the second-best book loses a lot of readers. So the market price of an orange is an excellent reflection of its true social value, whereas the bulk of Dan Brown's $20 million is only an excellent reflection of what he was able to divert from some other author to himself.

In other words, writing books (or creating artwork, or preserving artifacts) has important spillover effects. By writing this book, I imposed costs on some other author whose book you'd have been reading otherwise. But I didn't account for those costs when I decided to write it. It's quite possible that writing this book was a socially destructive act.

More explicitly: if this book is worth $20 to you, and the book you'd have read instead was worth $18, then I've improved your life $2 worth—and charged you $20 for the privilege! That means I'm way overpaid. And the treasures of Baghdad were probably way overvalued for exactly the same reason.

Global Warming, Local Crowding

Feeling guilty about your car's contribution to global warming? Feel guilty no longer; you can buy a TerraPass. Just go to http://www.terrapass.com and use the handy calculator to determine how much money you should send in to salve your conscience. The TerraPass people will use your contribution to fund clean-energy projects that cancel the equivalent of your car's carbon-dioxide emissions.

It's a cute idea and I applaud the sentiments behind it. But it completely misses several points.

First, carbon-dioxide emissions surely create spillover costs, and should surely be discouraged; that's a good reason to have gas taxes. But here TerraPass fails badly on two counts: first, it "taxes" only those who already feel guilty enough to buy a Terra-Pass; presumably those are precisely the people who already stop to think about the environmental consequences of a dash to the mall.

Second, unlike a gas tax, the TerraPass does absolutely nothing to raise the cost of driving *an additional mile*—which is precisely what it must do to get incentives right. The TerraPass calculator tells me that for my make and model of car, I should pay $49.95 a year if I drive less than 20,000 miles; $79.95 a year if I drive more. As I inch up from 10,000 miles to 12,000 to 15,000, I feel no additional costs whatsoever. But the whole point should be to make me feel the spillover costs of each and every mile that I drive.

Another problem is the TerraPass people's insistence on financing clean-energy projects, as opposed to projects with the largest possible social value. My $49.95 might (or might not) do a lot more good backing a garage band or invested in General Electric than supporting a clean-energy project.

Ideally, we should tax socially destructive activities and use the revenue in the most socially productive ways we can imagine. Ditto for pseudotaxes like the TerraPass. There's no reason alcohol taxes should be earmarked for alcoholism treatment, and there's no reason TerraPass revenue should be earmarked for environmental cleanup.

But the biggest objection to the TerraPass is that it singles out one relatively small spillover cost and ignores a much larger one. My carbon-dioxide emissions cause about $50 worth of damage each year. But my parking—on public streets where I take up valuable real estate—imposes far greater costs.

Apparently it took until 2006 for someone to notice that the social cost of mandated free and underpriced parking is nothing short of phenomenal, the implied subsidy being comparable to what we spend on Medicare or national defense. The someone who noticed is Professor Donald Shoup of UCLA, who wrote a deeply thoughtful book on the matter called *The High Cost of Free Parking*.

Urban on-street parking is almost always underpriced, which is why you can almost never find a spot. In many cases, it would be better to have no on-street parking at all, freeing up that real estate for expanded homes, shops, and cafés or additional driving lanes. Of course then it would be even harder to find a spot, but then a lot of people would switch to public transportation, which is all to the good.

It is crazy to feel guilty about dirtying the atmosphere without feeling even guiltier about clogging city streets. You might argue that global warming is a bigger problem than urban congestion, and you might be right. But that's not the issue. The issue is *your contribution* to global warming versus *your contribution* to urban congestion. And if you're a typical urban driver, the latter probably dwarfs the former.

Even if you never drive into the city, you're (at least indirectly) still part of the problem. Suburban shopping malls are almost everywhere required to have vastly oversized parking lots that are never close to full. You might not realize this, because you tend to search for spots in the close-in areas that *are* full. But the outlying areas sit idle, precluding the use of that land for anything of social value. And for every shopper who arrives by car, the mandated size of those lots gets bigger yet.

It's a fine thing to care whether you're damaging the environment, but it's also a fine thing to remember that our environment consists of more than just the air we breathe. It consists, too, of crowded sidewalks and vast empty parking lots. It might be good to have a TerraPass system for those with a broader perspective.

Or better yet, we could just price parking appropriately. As Professor Shoup points out, we already pay a high price for parking; it's just that we pay it indirectly "in our roles as consumers, investors, workers, residents, and taxpayers." If instead we paid directly in our role as motorists, we'd have an incentive to conserve the underlying scarce resource, namely parking spaces. Surely anyone who's concerned about the environment can see the nobility of that goal.

My Barnes and Noble Trade Deficit

To my vast delight, a Barnes and Noble superstore has arrived in Pittsford, New York, about a mile from my home in the neighboring town of Brighton. I shop at Barnes and Noble several times a week—mostly for books, sometimes for music, occasionally for software, and nearly always for coffee.

My trade deficit with Pittsford has grown explosively since Barnes and Noble arrived. In other words, I spend more money in Pittsford than I did before. A trade deficit is the amount you spend in a given place minus the amount you earn there. I don't earn any income in Pittsford, so my trade deficit is equal to the amount I spend.

I've been thinking about trade deficits because I picked up the local newspaper this morning and read an op-ed piece about the U.S. trade deficit with Mexico. It says that pre-NAFTA, the United States had a trade *surplus* with Mexico—the average American earned more in Mexico than he spent there. (Producing goods for sale to Mexicans counts as "earning in Mexico"; buying goods made by Mexicans counts as "spending in Mexico.") Today the opposite is true: the United States has a trade deficit with Mexico, and it's growing.

According to the op-ed piece, that's proof that the average American was better off without NAFTA. But the identical logic "proves" that I was better off without Barnes and Noble. Not only is the conclusion false; it's the exact opposite of the truth. When people take advantage of new opportunities to buy things they want, it usually makes them happier.

The truth is that *any* change in our trade position with respect to Mexico—in either direction—is evidence that free trade has been good for Americans. My neighbor got a job at the new Barnes and Noble. His trade *surplus* with Pittsford grew, just like my own trade *deficit*. In both cases, the changes meant that our lives had gotten better.

The same analogy illustrates another point: although NAFTA-induced *changes* in the U.S.-Mexican trade deficit are evidence of improvements, the actual *level* of the trade deficit means virtually nothing. If Barnes and Noble had located in the town of Penfield instead of Pittsford, I'd have a higher trade deficit with Penfield, a lower trade deficit with Pittsford, and my life would be about the same as it is now.

A more interesting number is my *overall* trade deficit—the total of all my spending minus the total of all my earning. My overall trade deficit was pretty high yesterday: I spent $600 on a living-room rug, and I earned $0. (It was a Sunday and I didn't feel like working.) My overall trade deficit was $600.

Traditionally, business journalists describe every increase in the overall trade deficit as a "worsening." According to that tradition, I had a very bad day yesterday. But it didn't *feel* like a bad day—I *like* my new rug, and it would have been inconvenient to put off buying it until a day when I felt like earning enough to pay for it.

When the nation's overall trade deficit increases, it means that Americans, on average, spent more than they earned. Maybe that's because your neighbors are behaving foolishly; maybe it's just because they have the good sense to realize that you can sometimes spend more than you earn—provided you're willing to draw down your savings.

In any event, foolishly excessive trade *surpluses* are a greater danger than foolishly excessive trade *deficits.* That's because excessive trade deficits are self-limiting: if you run a trade deficit every year, bankruptcy will eventually force you to stop. But excessive trade surpluses can go on forever. A perpetual trade surplus is likely to mean you're either working too hard or consuming too little; either way, you're not getting enough enjoyment out of life.

Here's the final thing to keep in mind when you read about the nation's overall trade deficit: the nation is nothing but the sum of individual households. But there are limits to how much you ought to care about what goes on in other people's households. Even if you are convinced that the average American spends too much, or earns too little, or spends too little, or earns too much, it's not entirely clear why it's any of your business. As long you have your own household in order, fretting about your neighbor's spending habits is a lot like fretting about the color of his living-room rug. Maybe lime green was a big mistake, but it's *his* mistake to live with.

An Outsourcing Fable

Once there was a man who invented a new and cheaper way to analyze MRI data. Medical costs fell, and more people got better care. The invention put some radiologists out of work, but even that had its upside—after a little retraining, the radiologists moved into other specialties where their talents were much appreciated.

Our inventor was hailed as a national hero—the new Thomas Edison. Oh, the radiologists grumbled, but almost everyone else recognized that you can't have progress without a bit of dislocation—just as candlemakers had once grumbled about Edison's electric lightbulb, but everyone else applauded it.

Soon the famous inventor was receiving MRI data from all over the country and running it through his marvelous new analyzing machine, the workings of which were shrouded in secrecy. But one day, an investigative reporter tracked down the inventor's disgruntled former assistant and learned that the great "invention" was nothing more than a $600 laptop computer connected to the Internet. The so-called inventor emailed data to Asia, where it was analyzed by low-paid Asian radiologists. They emailed back their reports, which he advertised as the output from his machine.

The nation was outraged. The man was not an inventor at all; he was nothing but an outsourcer! And all those American radiologists out of work! New York's Senator Chuck Schumer wrote an op-ed piece in the New York Times bemoaning the evils of outsourcing and using the fate of the radiologists as his prime example.

Somehow, everyone managed to overlook the fact that it didn't make a bit of difference whether the MRI data were being shipped to Asia or analyzed right on the inventor's desktop. The advantages of outsourcing were exactly the same as the advantages of the mythical invention. But in their rush to stem the evils of outsourcing, everyone lost track of those advantages.

That, of course, is a fable—an adaptation of a fable written long ago by Professor James Ingram of the University of North Carolina. But the fable overlaps with reality. It's true that in the near future Asian radiologists will be able to analyze MRI data over the Internet at a fraction of the current cost. And it's true that Senator Schumer had a recent op-ed piece in the *New York Times* decrying that development because it will mean fewer jobs for American radiologists.

Who would have expected to see a Democratic senator protesting a genuine reduction in medical costs that's good for just about everyone, except a group of highly paid specialists who might have to retrain if they want to stay socially useful? In the same article, Senator Schumer speaks out on behalf of $150,000-a-year American software engineers who face competition from Asians who can do the same job for $20,000 a year. It is a sure bet that the consumers who will benefit from that competition earn, on average, far less than $150,000. But rather than rejoice for those consumers, the senator takes his stand with a small group of highly paid professionals who would prefer to continue being highly paid, even as they continue working in an area where their skills are no longer needed.

Obviously, Senator Schumer does not understand the moral of our fable. Just to spell it out for him, the moral is this: outsourcing work is, from an economic point of view, *exactly the same thing* as discovering a new technology. If you can ship your problems abroad and have them come back solved, that's exactly as good as feeding your problems to a new kind of machine and having solutions pop out the other end. New trading patterns, like new inventions, can require some social adjustment, but the benefits almost always outweigh the costs. If you cheer for progress, then you must cheer for trade.

The New Racism

Not long ago in American history, political platforms contained phrases like: "Federal contracts, whenever possible, should be performed by white workers." Politicians demanded tax incentives to reward firms for hiring whites instead of blacks. Those same politicians endorsed "Right-to-Know" legislation to alert consumers when products were produced by the "wrong" kind of workers. They embraced slogans like "Buy white!"

When I say this kind of thing was commonplace "not long ago," I really *mean* not long ago. Except for one morally insignificant difference, I got all of the above from John Kerry's Web site. The only change I made is this: where Kerry said "American," I substituted "white."

But I don't mean to single out either Senator Kerry or Democrats in general. Both major parties (and most of the minor ones) are infested with protectionist fellow travelers, who would discriminate on the basis of national origin no less virulently than David Duke or any other overt racist would discriminate on the basis of skin color. But if racism is morally repugnant—and it is—then so is xenophobia, and for exactly the same reasons.

Now hold on a minute, you might say. Isn't the U.S. government elected by Americans to serve Americans? Indeed, don't governments exist in the first place for the express purpose of favoring their own citizens? The U.S. Army discriminates by defending American soil more vigorously than the soil of, say, Peru. We discriminate against Icelanders by locating our interstate highways in North America for our own convenience, rather than in Reykjavik for theirs. So why shouldn't American government policies favor American workers at the expense of foreigners?

Well, sure, the U.S. government is elected by Americans to serve Americans. There was a time when a lot of Southern sheriffs could have said they'd been elected by white citizens to serve white citizens. It does not follow that it's okay to run roughshod over the rights of everyone else.

As for defense and interstate highways, these are great collective undertakings. We pay for them through our taxes. It makes sense that those who pay the costs should reap the benefits. It is no more inappropriate for the U.S. Army to defend Americans instead of Peruvians than it is for Burger King to provide food for Burger King customers instead of McDonald's customers.

But the labor market isn't like that at all. When General Motors hires an American in Detroit or a Mexican in Ciudad Juárez, the rest of us are not footing the bill. And that makes it none of our business. Nor should we want it to be.

I hold this truth to be self-evident: it is just plain ugly to care more about total strangers in Detroit than about total strangers in Juárez. Of course we care most about the people closest to us—our families more than our friends, and our friends more than our acquaintances. But once you start talking about total strangers, they all ought to be on pretty much the same footing. I sometimes hear Americans say, "I care more about Americans than Mexicans because I have more in common with Americans." If you happen to be white, you could just as well say you care more about white strangers than black strangers because you've got more in common with whites. Does that make it okay to punish firms for hiring blacks?

Anyway, protectionism doesn't work; laws intended to "protect" Americans might raise wages, but they raise the prices of the goods we buy even more, leaving us worse off. The proof of this fact (and it is indeed a fact, not an opinion—one which is as well established among economists as Darwinian evolution is among biologists) can be found in any intermediate textbook on microeconomics. The key insight is that finding a new trading partner is exactly like finding a new technology; there is no fundamental difference between having your MRI data analyzed by an Indian over the Internet and having your MRI data analyzed by clever new software that runs directly on your laptop. If technology makes us richer, then so must trade.

But that observation is quite tangential to my main point here, which is that even if protectionism *did* work—even if Kerry-style (or Nader-style or Buchanan-style) protectionism *could* improve Americans' well-being at the expense of foreigners—it would still be wrong.

If you support protectionism because you think it's good for *you*, you've probably just got your economics wrong. But if you support protectionism because you think it's good for your fellow Americans, at the expense of foreigners, then it seems to me you've got your morals wrong too.

Granted, this book is supposed to be about economics, not morality, and your moral standards might be very different from mine. But indulge me for a moment: if it's okay to enrich ourselves by denying foreigners the right to earn a living, why shouldn't we enrich ourselves by invading peaceful countries and seizing their assets? Most of us don't think that's a good idea, and not just because it might backfire. We don't think it's a good idea because we believe human beings have human rights, whatever their color and wherever they live. Stealing assets is wrong, and so is stealing the right to earn a living, no matter where the victim was born.

FIFTEEN
MATTERS OF LIFE
AND DEATH

In 2006, Dallas newspapers reported that Tirhas Habtegiris, a 27-year-old patient at Baylor Regional Medical Center, had been removed from her ventilator because she couldn't pay her medical bills. According to the newspapers, the hospital gave Ms. Habtegiris ten days' notice, and then, with the bills still unpaid, withdrew her life support on the eleventh day. It took Ms. Habtegiris about fifteen minutes to die.

Bloggers, most notably "YucatanMan" at *Daily Kos,* rose up in anger over the reported fact that "economic considerations," as opposed to what the bloggers call "compassion," drove the decision to unplug Ms. Habtegiris. Before long, Baylor responded with a statement denying that economic considerations played any role in the decision, which, according to Baylor, was made without regard to any cost-benefit analysis.

I devoutly hope that Baylor's denial was a lie. "Cost-benefit analysis," after all, is just a fancy phrase for "considering the consequences." What moral monster would unplug a woman from a ventilator without regard to the consequences?

One consequence you might want to consider is that by unplugging Ms. Habtegiris you make the ventilator available for someone else. The more critical the needs of that someone else, the more willing you should be to unplug her. That's cost-benefit analysis. It's also—and you can check with that someone else's relatives if you don't believe me—an expression of compassion.

Compassion and economic considerations are never in conflict, because they're both about meeting people's needs. For example, if you ask people—and especially poor people—what their most dire needs are, you'll find that "guaranteed ventilator support" ranks pretty low on the list. Okay, I haven't actually done a survey, but I'm going out on a limb here and predicting that something like, say, milk, is going to rank a lot higher up the priority list than ventilator insurance.

When I speak of "ventilator insurance," I'm not talking about a formal contract with monthly premiums; I'm talking about a societal commitment to keep people on ventilators even when they can't pay their bills. YucatanMan and other bloggers took it for granted that a compassionate society must supply that kind of ventilator insurance. I say just the opposite.

The back of my envelope says that a lifetime's worth of ventilator insurance costs society somewhere around $75. (I got this number by multiplying the cost of providing a ventilator times the probability you'll eventually need one.) I'm going to hazard a guess that if, on her twenty-first birthday, you'd asked Tirhas Habtegiris to select her own $75 present, she wouldn't have asked for ventilator insurance. She might have chosen $75 worth of groceries; she might have chosen a new pair of shoes; she might have chosen a few dozen iTunes downloads. But not ventilator insurance.

There is nothing compassionate about giving someone the wrong present. There is nothing compassionate about giving ventilator insurance to someone who prefers milk and eggs. One might even say that choosing to ignore other people's preferences is precisely the opposite of compassion.

There is room for a great deal of disagreement about how much assistance rich people should give to poor people, either voluntarily or through the tax system. But surely whatever we do spend should be spent in the ways that are most helpful.

Therefore there's no use arguing that the real trade-off should not be ventilators versus milk but ventilators versus tax cuts, or ventilators versus foreign wars. It's one thing to say we should spend more to help the poor, but quite another to say that what we're currently spending should be spent ineffectively.

The bloggers at *Daily Kos* would have us guarantee ventilator support to everyone who can't afford it. For the same cost, we could give each of those people a choice between ventilator insurance or $75 cash. If it turns out that I'm wrong and they all want the ventilator insurance, so be it. But why not at least ask them?

Tirhas Habtegiris would probably have taken the cash. Then she'd have gotten sick and regretted her decision. And then we as a society would have been in exactly the same position as before—deciding whether to foot the bill to keep Ms. Habtegiris alive a little longer.

At that point, there's a powerful human instinct to come to the rescue. Well, more precisely, there's a powerful human instinct to demand that someone *else* come to the rescue. (I'm guessing that in the wake of the Habtegiris case, nobody at *Daily Kos* has taken to funding ventilator insurance for the poor.) Be that as it may, choices have to be made. A policy of helping everyone who needs a ventilator *is* a policy of spending less to help the same class of people in other ways. I'd rather help them in other ways.

When I said as much in the pages of *Slate,* Robert Frank took me to task in his *New York Times* column for "completely ignor[ing] moral emotions like sympathy and empathy." Professor Frank believes the government should supply ventilator services to poor people. But you can't supply more ventilator services without buying more ventilators. So Professor Frank's position, in essence, is that if he had $1 million to spend helping poor people, he'd spend it on a couple of ventilators. Myself, I'd be more likely to buy milk and eggs.

Remarkably, Professor Frank admits that most poor people would prefer the milk and eggs, but still argues for the ventilators on the grounds that it would make the rest of us feel better! But ignoring other people's needs to make yourself feel better is the very opposite of sympathy and empathy.

Accounting for "economic considerations" means—by definition—trying to give people what they'll value the most. In other words, it is from economic considerations that true compassion flows.

Many years ago, the Nobel laureate Thomas Schelling asked why communities will sometimes spend millions to save the life of a known victim—say, a trapped miner—but refuse to spend even, say, $200,000 on a highway guardrail that would save an average of one life per year. His answer was to distinguish between "identified lives"—like the trapped miner, or Tirhas Habtegiris—and "statistical lives," like the unknown beneficiaries of the guardrail. Robert Frank embraces this distinction. For some reason, we are supposed to care more about identified lives than statistical lives, and somehow, all of this is supposed to be a justification for giving people ventilators when they prefer milk.

But the distinction between a statistical and an identified life is incoherent, morally obtuse, and impossible to maintain. First, it's incoherent: at what point does a life pass from being statistical to being identified? I've just heard on the news that there's a miner trapped in West Virginia. At the moment, I know nothing about him, so I suppose his is a statistical life. When does that life become identified? When I learn his name? When I learn his children's names? When I learn what town he lived in? There's simply no clear line.

You might say he becomes identified at the moment he gets trapped in the mine, but that's equally arbitrary. I knew yesterday that of the ten thousand people working in West Virginia mines, it was virtually certain that at least one would eventually be trapped. I had no idea who that person would be. Today I know there's a miner trapped and I have no idea who he is. That doesn't seem like a substantially different circumstance.

Likewise, I know in advance, pretty much with certainty, that x number of people will need life support this year. There is a certain amount I am willing to pay to provide that support. According to Professors Schelling and Frank, that amount should rise—when, exactly? When I learn their names? When I learn their children's names?

Besides being incoherent, the distinction between a statistical and an identified life is morally obtuse. Why on earth should I care more about one stranger than another just because I happen to know their names—or whatever else your criterion might be? If for $1 million I can save a stranger on a ventilator about whom I know everything, or ten strangers in a mine about whom I know nothing, I will save the ten statistical lives over the one identified life every time. And it seems to me to be morally reprehensible to choose otherwise.

Yes, I realize there's a powerful instinct to pour resources into the person you know something about. I even think I know how that instinct evolved: for most of human history, the people we knew the most about tended to be our closest relatives. But in the age of the Internet, that's no longer true, and the caveman instinct to prefer identified lives is as antiquated as the caveman instinct to fling feces at anyone who irritates you.

Finally, the distinction between a statistical and an identified life would be impossible to maintain even if you wanted to. You simply cannot have a policy of spending no more than $200,000 to save lives in general and up to $10 million to save lives in particular, because every life in general eventually becomes a life in particular. If we are willing to pay up to $200,000 per person to save the hundred people we know will need life support later this year, and then up to $10 million per person after we learn their names, we might as well have agreed to spend $10 million per person up front.

The identified/statistical life approach says, in essence, that I should prefer three deaths to one death as long as the three victims happen to be invisible. I'd prefer to live in a world where people try to help other people (especially poor people) in the ways that people want to be helped, and where the value of your life does not depend on whether I happen to know who you are.*

---

* More than one clever economist has tried to defend favoring identified lives by observing that one rescue from certain death is worth more (to the victim) than 100 rescues from 1% chances of death. I do not believe this argument is correct, and I've explained why not in a technical note on my Web site at http://www.landsburg.com/lives.pdf.

* * *

If I could save you $5 in taxes by releasing a toxic chemical that might kill you—say with a probability of one in a million—I wouldn't do it. If I could save you $20 in taxes by releasing the same chemical, I probably would.

That's because I'm looking out for your interests. For this size risk, I happen to know that most people would rather be safe than be $5 richer, but most people would rather be $20 richer than be safe.

I know this because economists have made a habit of observing people's choices—for example, the size of the pay cuts they'll accept to move into safer jobs. On that basis, Harvard Law professor Kip Viscusi estimates that the average American will pay about $5 to steer clear of a one-in-a-million chance of being killed. For blue-collar women, it's closer to $7, and for blue-collar men it's even higher.

(Yes, blue-collar workers will pay more for safety than white-collar workers. It's not clear why, but that's what the data show.)

Economists summarize Viscusi's findings by saying that the average American life is worth about $5 million. There are other ways to measure the value of a life: a chemist might calculate the market value of the compounds that make up your body, an accountant might calculate the present value of your future earnings, or a theologian might pronounce that your life is priceless. Depending on what problem you're out to solve, any one of these calculations might be relevant. When you're out to solve the problem of making people happier, however, it's often the economist's calculation that counts.

Your life is probably worth somewhere between five and ten million dollars. Let's round up and call it ten. That doesn't mean you'd sell me your life for that price; I doubt you'd sell it for ten times as much. It's just a measure of how much you'll willingly pay to avoid small risks. But for a lot of policy questions, that's exactly what we want to measure.

If King Kong is likely to kill 300 Americans out of 300 million, there's a one in a million chance you'll be a victim. If we can stop him with $300 million worth of ape repellent—that is, $1 million per life—your share of the tax bill comes to about a dollar. That's a good deal.

But if instead it costs $30 billion to stop Kong, then it's better to let him wreak havoc. Your share of that $30 billion would be $100, and we know from Professor Viscusi's studies that almost nobody wants to pay that much to avoid a one-in-a-million chance of death. By letting Kong run rampant, we're respecting your preferences—and making you as happy as it's possible to be in a world where giant apes run wild.

In reality, we are not threatened by giant apes, but we are threatened by terrorists, auto accidents, street crime, and environmental catastrophes. How much will a reasonable government spend to reduce these risks? The answer is: as much as people want them to, but not more. Roughly, that's $10 million per life.

Click and Clack, the Tappet Brothers of National Public Radio's *Car Talk*, have failed to digest that calculation. The Tappets have declared war on drivers with cell phones. Their weapon is moral suasion, liberally buttressed with illogic and untruths. Their targets are not just drivers but legislators; the Tappets (real names: Tom and Ray Magliozzi) want bans on cell-phone use by drivers in all fifty states. So far, they've met their goal in exactly zero (though some states have enacted "hands-free" laws).

Talking while driving is deadly; of this, there is much evidence and little doubt. Cell-phone use increases your accident risk by almost 400 percent. But so what? It's a big and unwarranted leap from "talking while driving is deadly" to "talking while driving is bad." After all, lots of things are deadly without being bad. Take driving itself, for example. Just getting behind the wheel (as opposed to staying home in bed) multiplies your accident risk by far more than 400 percent, but so far the Tappets have not proposed to outlaw driving.

Presumably that's because they recognize that the benefits of driving exceed the costs, even though the costs include tens of thousands of fatalities in this country every year (and even though the costs are not entirely borne by the people who reap the benefits). In other words, the Tappets implicitly recognize that cost-benefit analysis is a legitimate basis for public policy. So you might think they would welcome a cost-benefit analysis of cell-phone use by drivers, at least as a starting point for discussion. Instead, when just such an analysis came along, the Tappets responded with vitriol and lies.

The analysis is courtesy of Brookings Institution economists Robert Hahn, Paul Tetlock, and Jason Burnett, who reckon that drivers' cell phones are indeed deadly but nevertheless (on balance) a good thing. Personally, I'm unconvinced, for reasons I'll get to. But at least theirs is a serious attempt to analyze a difficult problem. The Tappet brothers, however, are offended by the very notion that anyone would attempt to think about such matters. On their Web page, the Tappets dismiss the Brookings study thusly: "Here's an economic analysis that shows the enormous value to the economy of driving and talking. (As long as we don't factor in the injuries, lost lives, pain, and suffering of all those accidents, that is!)"

On the contrary, the Hahn-Tetlock-Burnett study is all *about* factoring in the injuries, lost lives, pain, and suffering from cell-phone-related accidents. The researchers estimate that in one year, driver use of cell phones caused about 300 fatalities, 38,000 nonfatal injuries, and 200,000 damaged vehicles. Their goal is to weigh those costs against the benefits to drivers of using their phones.

In a letter to the *New York Times,* the Tappet brothers referred to one of those 300 fatalities—a two-and-a-half-year-old girl named Morgan Lee—and asked, "What price has Mr. Hahn plugged into his nice, clean, economic model to account for the misery and tears that such outright selfishness has wrought?" If they'd bothered to read the research they're so quick to criticize—and they're both MIT grads, so it shouldn't be beyond them—they'd have found the answer: the price is $6.6 million, a widely used standard based on Kip Viscusi's analysis. (I rounded this number up to ten million when we were talking about King Kong.)

If putting a dollar value on human lives strikes you as cold-hearted, grow up. You implicitly put a dollar value on human lives every time you buy a candy bar with funds that could instead have been donated to the local fire department. No matter who you are, there is a limit to what you're willing to spend to save lives; the only question is whether you're willing to think honestly about what that limit is. Viscusi thought hard not about his own limit but about how to measure other people's limits, through observations of their behavior. That's where the $6.6 million comes from—it's an estimate of what real people in real situations are willing to pay to make themselves safer.

Pricing the fatalities at $6.6 million each, and adding in the costs of injuries and vehicle damage, Mr. Hahn and his colleagues estimate that in one year, cell-phone use by drivers caused $4.6 billion worth of damage. That's the cost of letting drivers use cell phones. It's a pretty big cost. But not everything that's costly is bad. To figure out whether it's bad, you've got to weigh the costs against the benefits.

Here's how you measure the relevant benefits: the value of a cell-phone call is equal to what you're willing to pay for it, minus what you actually pay for it. Willingness to pay is estimated from demand studies (factoring in the truism that some calls are worth more than others). Actual charges, of course, come from real-life cell-phone bills. From that kind of calculation, Hahn and his colleagues conclude that in one year, cell-phone calls made by drivers had a total value of $25 billion. That $25 billion benefit beats the $4.6 billion cost, so—according to Hahn and his colleagues—cell phones for drivers are, in the end, a good thing.

Actually, I don't buy it, for a variety of reasons. First, drivers make a lot of calls that could easily wait for the next rest stop. Those calls shouldn't count as benefits of talking while driving, because they would be placed even if talking while driving were banned. So—as Hahn et al acknowledge in a note near the end of their paper—the true benefit of talking while driving is probably far less than $25 billion. They still believe it's well over $4.6 billion, but at this point they're guessing.

Moreover, Hahn et al missed a potentially important factor on the cost side: they counted fatalities, they counted injuries, they counted property damage, but they failed to account for the inconvenience to people who choose not to drive because cell phones have made driving more dangerous. Those people aren't killed or injured, so they don't show up in statistics, but they are bearing real costs.

So I have no idea whether talking while driving is a good thing or a bad thing. Unlike the Tappet brothers, however, I'd want to think about that question before enacting legislation.

And the numbers really do matter. Suppose that after reworking Hahn's argument, we were to discover that the cost of a ban is, say, $10 billion. Then what would the Tappets' cherished ban accomplish? Drivers would give up $10 billion in benefits to prevent 300 deaths (plus some injuries and property damage). That's a lousy deal, *by the standards of the very people who are being killed.* At that price, most people would prefer to risk being among the unlucky 300 rather than give up their cell phones.

On the other hand, maybe the cost of a ban is only $1 billion. In that case, the ban's a good idea. So it's well worthwhile for someone to get these numbers right. Hahn and his colleagues have at least made a foray in that direction, and one hopes that more careful studies will follow.

Over two centuries ago, a lawyer named William Blackstone declared that it's better for ten guilty persons to escape than for one innocent to suffer. Why ten, as opposed to, say, twelve or eight? Because Blackstone said so, that's why. By pulling the number ten out of thin air, Blackstone defiantly refused to think about the trade-offs that go into designing a criminal justice system. But for two centuries, legal scholars have cited Blackstone's *refusal* to think and mistaken it for an example of a *thought*.

Of *course* it's a bad thing to convict the innocent. We all know that, just as we know it's a bad thing to acquit the guilty. The hard part is deciding how many false acquittals you're willing to accept to avoid a false conviction. That number matters. It matters whether it is ten or twelve or eight, because every time we rewrite a criminal statute or modify the rules of evidence, we're adjusting the terms of that trade-off—so it's got to be worth thinking about what terms to aim for.

That means thinking about costs. The cost (to you) of a false conviction is that you might be the unlucky innocent who goes to jail. The cost (to you) of a false acquittal is that you might cross paths with the criminal we just freed (or with some other criminal who's feeling emboldened by all these false acquittals). A "ten guilty men" standard saddles you with one bundle of risks; a "five guilty men" or a "hundred guilty men" standard saddles you with another. The right standard is the one that saddles you with the burden you prefer (where "prefer" means "dislike the least"). Or better yet, since we all have to live by the same rules, the right standard is the one that most of us prefer.

In that light, "ten guilty men" seems like far too strict a standard. Ten false acquittals in murder cases give you ten chances to cross paths with a newly released murderer. One false conviction gives you one chance of landing (at worst) in the electric chair. I'm not so fond of either prospect, but given a choice, I'll take the latter. And though I could be wrong, I'll bet just about anyone else would too. I expect we'd all be happier with, say, a "three guilty men" standard: if we're 75 percent sure you did the crime, you do the time. Three times out of four we're right, one time out of four we're wrong, and four times out of four we're okay with those odds.

In some cases we'll be 80 percent sure or 90 percent sure or 95 percent sure, and we'll like those odds even better. The cutoff for reasonable doubt should be at the odds we find just barely acceptable.

You could of course say something silly like: "No, I will never be satisfied as long as there's any chance at all of sending an innocent man to jail." I could respond with something equally silly like: "Well, *I* will never be satisfied as long as there's any chance at all of freeing a killer who might kill again." Unless we dispense with criminal justice entirely, or preemptively jail the entire population, neither of those criteria will ever be met. We *will* make mistakes, and we ought to think hard about which combination of mistakes is most tolerable. It's usually suboptimal to specialize in just one kind of mistake. If you never miss a plane, you're spending too much time in airports; if you never convict an innocent, you're not convicting enough of the guilty.

So I would be comfortable with a 75 percent standard for reasonable doubt, at least in a world of scrupulously honest policemen. But I am substantially less comfortable with it in a world where policemen (and others) sometimes manufacture evidence against people they don't like (or fail to pursue evidence that might exonerate a convenient scapegoat). That makes me want to nudge the cutoff up a bit, probably to something very like Blackstone's ninety-something-percent standard. So maybe he got it right after all. But it still would have been better if he'd thought about it.

If we execute murderers, why not execute the people who write computer worms? According to the math on the back of my envelope, it would be a better investment.

First, what's the value of executing a murderer? A high-end estimate is that each execution deters about ten murders (the highest estimate I've ever seen is twenty-four, but the closest thing to a consensus estimate in the econometric literature is about eight). So call it ten lives saved, with a value—again a high-end estimate—of about $10 million apiece. Then the benefit of executing a murderer is roughly ten times $10 million, or $100 million—and that's probably too high.*

---

* If you think I've overestimated the deterrent effect, that's fine; adjust it downward and the argument to follow gets stronger, not weaker.

Compare that to the benefit of executing the author of a computer worm, virus, or Trojan horse. There seems to be no good name for such people, so I've made one up: I call them *vermiscriptors*. It's estimated that vermiscripting and related activities cost the world about $50 billion a year.

Now let me be clear that when I say "it's estimated," what I mean is, "somebody said this on the Internet." There are a lot of reasons to believe the number is seriously overblown, not least because victimized firms tend to exaggerate the damage when they're making insurance claims. But let's go with this number for the sake of argument; we can always modify it later.

Given that $50 billion figure, all we'd have to do is deter just one-fifth of one percent of all vermiscripting for just one year in order to gain the same $100 million benefit we get from executing a killer. Anything over one-fifth of one percent, and any effects that linger beyond the first year are just gravy.

So much for the benefits. What about costs? The cost of an execution is one life—usually (one hopes) the life of someone guilty, but occasionally the life of a wrongly convicted innocent. The question is: which is worth more, the life of the average convicted murderer or the life of the average convicted vermiscriptor?

Plausibly, the latter. Compared to murderers, vermiscriptors might be easier to rehabilitate and probably have more in the way of skills that can be put to good use. (Offsetting this, though, is the prospect that those same skills can be put to further *bad* use.) Let's bias things very strongly in the vermiscriptor's favor by valuing the average murderer's life at zero and the average vermiscriptor's life at $100 million—the same value we earlier attributed to *ten* lives.

That, of course, should make us more reluctant to execute

the vermiscriptor. Even so, executing the vermiscriptor might still beat executing a murderer. If one execution can deter $200 million worth of computerized vandalism, we've covered the $100 million cost of the vermiscriptor's life and still come out ahead. That's still just two-fifths of one percent of one year's worth of virus damage—and still a plausibly easy hurdle to clear.

Conclusion: on a pure cost-benefit basis, we should be quicker to execute a vermiscriptor than a murderer. But of course we're not. Which raises the question: why not?

Here's one answer: "These things can't possibly be reduced to numbers. Who cares if some economist said a human life was worth $7 million or $8 million or $10 million? You might find these numbers interesting in some abstract academic sort of way, but they have nothing at all to do with making wise policy decisions."

The problem with that answer is that it's wrong. If we can deter one random murder in America, we make you a little bit safer: your chance of being a murder victim shrinks by about 1 in 300 million (because that's how many Americans there are). If we can execute one killer and deter ten random murders, the enhancement to your safety is multiplied by ten: your chance of being a victim shrinks by 1 in 30 million. When we say that your life is worth $10 million, we mean precisely that you'd be willing to pay about one 30-millionth of $10 million—about 33 cents—for that much extra safety. (Actually, you'd probably be willing to pay slightly less, because each execution, while making you safer on the street, also enhances the risk that you yourself will be falsely convicted and executed someday.)

On the other hand, suppose we can execute one vermiscriptor and thereby eliminate, oh, say, 1 percent of all computer viruses for one year. Assuming that half the $50 billion cost of malicious hacking is concentrated in the United States and that you bear your proportionate share of that cost, we're putting about 83 cents in your pocket. Which would you rather have, the safety or the cash? Almost every American would take the cash; that's exactly what we learn from studies like Kip Viscusi's.

Executing the murderer means giving you the safety. Executing the vermiscriptor means giving you the cash. You'd rather have the cash than the safety. Ergo, executing the vermiscriptor is the better policy.

There's at least one exception to this reasoning: maybe there's an alternative and less drastic punishment that is highly effective against vermiscriptors and not against murderers. If we can effectively deter malicious hackers by cutting off their supply of Twinkies or crippling their EverQuest avatars, then there's no need to fry them. Whether that would work is an empirical question.

Of course, this is all very back-of-the-envelope. As I've already acknowledged, I pulled the $50 billion figure for vermiscriptor-induced damage off the Internet, which may be slightly less reliable than pulling it out of thin air. All my other numbers were approximations, too—some better than others. (Some might argue that I also omitted the moral costs and benefits of capital punishment, or that capital punishment is better justified by retribution than by deterrence. As for me, I hold that the government's job is to improve our lives, not to impose its morality.)

So while I'm not prepared to defend these particular numbers terribly vigorously, I *am* prepared to defend this way of *using* the numbers. Governments exist largely to supply protections that, for one reason or another, we can't purchase in the marketplace. Those governments perform best when they supply the protections we value most. We can measure their performance only if we are willing to calculate costs and benefits and to respect what our calculations tell us, even when it's counterintuitive. Any policymaker who won't do this kind of arithmetic is fundamentally unserious about policy.

SIXTEEN
THINGS THAT MAKE
ME SQUIRM

Once upon a time, an economics professor named Randall Wright resigned his job at Cornell and drove his Dodge Daytona Turbo down to Philadelphia to begin teaching at the University of Pennsylvania. When Professor Wright found out how much Philadelphians pay to insure their cars (typically over $3,600 a year for a married man over 25), he gave up driving.

If you live in Philadelphia, your auto insurance probably costs about three times what it would in Milwaukee and more than twice what it would in Seattle. Philadelphians have traditionally paid more for insurance than their counterparts in Baltimore, Chicago, and Cleveland, despite much higher theft rates in those other cities. This led Professor Wright to ask a question that ultimately became the provocative title for an article in the prestigious *American Economic Review:* "Why Is Automobile Insurance in Philadelphia So Damn Expensive?"

A reasonable first guess is that the answer has little to do with economics and much to do with the behavior of state regulatory agencies. But the facts don't support that guess. Pittsburgh is in the same state as Philadelphia, and Professor Wright could have insured his car in Pittsburgh for less than half the Philadelphia price, even though Pittsburgh's theft rate was more than double Philadelphia's. Other states provide equally striking contrasts: San Jose is much cheaper than neighboring San Francisco; Jacksonville is much cheaper than Miami; Kansas City is much cheaper than St. Louis.

While Professor Wright was puzzling over these discrepancies, a Penn graduate student named Eric Smith was involved in an auto accident. The other driver was at fault, but he had few assets and no insurance, so Smith had to collect from his own insurer. That unpleasant experience gave Smith and Wright the insight that led to a new theory of insurance pricing.

In brief, the theory is that uninsured drivers cause high premiums, and high premiums cause uninsured drivers. In somewhat more detail, a plethora of uninsured drivers increases the chance that, like Mr. Smith, you'll have to collect from your own insurer even when you're not at fault; to compensate for that risk, insurers charge higher premiums. But when premiums are high, more people opt against buying insurance, thereby creating a plethora of uninsured drivers and completing the vicious circle. Once a city enters that vicious circle, it can't escape.

In other words, insurance rates are driven by self-fulfilling prophecies. If everyone expects a lot of uninsured drivers, insurers charge high premiums, so many drivers choose to be uninsured. Conversely, if everyone expects most drivers to be insured, insurers charge low premiums, so more drivers buy insurance. Either outcome is self-reinforcing. A city that falls into either category (for whatever random reasons) remains there indefinitely.

So it's possible that modern Philadelphians are paying an exorbitant price for a brief outbreak of pessimism among their grandparents. If, for just one brief moment, and contrary to all past evidence, Philadelphians could believe that insurance rates will fall and their neighbors will become insured, that belief alone could cause insurance rates to fall and the neighbors to become insured. And then forever after, Philadelphia's insurance market might look like Milwaukee's.

Or maybe not; the Milwaukee-style outcome will be undermined if Philadelphia is home to enough of the "hardcore uninsured," who are unwilling to insure themselves even at Milwaukee prices. The Smith-Wright theory predicts that some cities, but not all cities, have the potential to maintain low insurance premiums in the long run.

But in cases where that potential exists, it would be nice to see it realized. One way to accomplish that is by enforcing mandatory insurance laws. (Smith and Wright point out that *enacting* a mandatory insurance law, which a majority of the states have already done, is not the same as *enforcing* a mandatory insurance law, which is nearly unheard of. Moreover, even where the laws are enforced, minimum liability limits are typically very low, and probably too low to make much difference.)

In theory, mandatory insurance could make life better for *everyone,* including those who currently prefer to be uninsured. Philadelphians who are unwilling to buy insurance for $3,500 might welcome the opportunity to buy insurance for $500. So if mandatory insurance yields a dramatic drop in premiums, then both the previously insured and the newly insured can benefit. (In practice, there will probably be a small segment of the population—presumably at the low end of the income distribution— who will be unhappy about having to buy insurance even at $500. But income-based insurance subsidies would allow even the poorest of the poor to share the benefits of lower premiums.)

For ideological free marketeers (like myself), theories like Smith and Wright's can be intellectually jarring. We are accustomed to defending free markets as the guarantors of both liberty and prosperity, but here's a case where liberty and prosperity are at odds: by forcing people to act against their own self-interest in the short run, governments can make *everybody* more prosperous in the long run. (Though some libertarians will object that the prosperity is an illusion, because governments that have been empowered to make us more prosperous will inevitably abuse that power to our detriment.)

Is it worth sacrificing a small amount of freedom for cheaper auto insurance? I am inclined to believe that the answer is yes, but the question makes me squirm a bit.

Most of the time, we're not forced to choose between prosperity and economic freedom, because the two go hand in hand. Canada's Fraser Institute, in cooperation with several dozen think tanks around the world, assigns each country an economic freedom rating from 1 to 10. High ratings go to countries with limited government, low taxes, well-enforced property rights, functioning markets, and free trade. Currently, Hong Kong ranks first, followed by Singapore, and then we have a three-way tie among New Zealand, Switzerland, and the United States. Myanmar brings up the rear. A scatter plot of economic freedom versus income per capita, with each black dot representing a country, is shown on the next page.

(I've omitted the dot for Luxembourg, which, with its per capita income of almost $70,000 per year, would have forced me to rescale the entire graph.) The general upward trend is obvi-

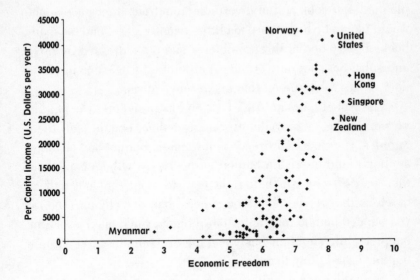

ous. Of course that doesn't prove anything about causation, but it's awfully suggestive—and we have plenty of theory to support that suggestion.

Incidentally, if you carry out the same experiment with *political* freedom—including scheduled elections, robust opposition parties, freedom of speech and religion, and so forth—on the horizontal axis, the dots look almost completely random. Political freedom is, in my opinion, a good thing, but unlike economic freedom it seems to have almost no link to prosperity.

For those of us who care about both (economic) freedom and prosperity, it's a stroke of good fortune that our goals are so frequently in harmony. For the most part, freedom promotes prosperity. But not always. The car-insurance market in Philadelphia is an exception. In fact, this book has been mostly about exceptions. Cost-benefit analysis tells me that the world has too little casual sex (at least among the least promiscuous), too few people, either too much or too little beauty (because beautiful people are fun to look at, but divert attention from other people who would like to be looked at), too little inventiveness, and too many books. Every one of those problems can be addressed by taxes and subsidies, but only at the expense of a little economic freedom. That's the trade-off that makes me squirm.

The Nobel laureate Amartya Sen has posed an even starker version of the same trade-off: Suppose some people (call them "prudes") cherish their freedom of religion, but not half so much as they would cherish a ban on pornography. Others (call them the "lewds") cherish their right to read smut, but not half so much as they would cherish a general ban on religion. Then if you banned both pornography *and* religion, you'd make everyone happier while simultaneously making everyone less free. Would that be a good thing to do?

Sen's dilemma is unlikely to arise in practice because there will always be people who are offended by book banning, so a ban can't make *everyone* happier. But in practice we don't judge policies by their ability to garner unanimous support. Instead, we adopt more flexible criteria like the cost-benefit principle: a policy is good when its benefits exceed its costs, with benefits (or costs) measured by what the proponents (or opponents) would be willing to pay to see the policy enacted (or defeated).

Unfortunately, that's no help in terms of dodging Sen's dilemma, which simply reasserts itself in the cost-benefit context. Suppose I'm willing to pay $20 to read the subversive works of Paul Krugman and you're willing to pay $40 to stop me. A strict cost-benefit analysis suggests that Krugman's writing should be banned. (There's no need for a ban if you can locate me and offer me, say, $30 to change my reading habits—and if you can be assured that I won't just take the money and run. But let's suppose the impracticality of such arrangements leaves book banning as the only realistic alternative.)

That's a conclusion most of us find repugnant, and it would be nice to avoid it. One way out is simply to declare that "psychic costs don't count." If you don't like getting your nose punched, your aversion goes into the cost-benefit calculus and inspires us to write laws that discourage nose punching. But if you don't like knowing I read Krugman, that's your own problem.

Appealing as that position might sound, it's also distressingly incoherent. If my habit of reading Krugman and my habit of punching your nose are equally painful to you, why should public policy discourage one and not the other?

One answer is that psychic costs shouldn't count because they're too easy to exaggerate. Anyone can claim to have suffered $1 million worth of emotional distress, but we have no way of knowing which claims are simply fabricated. Another answer is that once you start counting psychic harm, people start training themselves to feel it.

Neither answer strikes me as fully satisfactory. Still, my gut tells me that psychic harm shouldn't count. On the other hand, this is the same gut that keeps telling me to go ahead and have another brownie, so I'm not sure how much I should trust it.

The mirror image of a psychic cost is a psychic benefit. When the Army Corps of Engineers executed a cost-benefit analysis of undamming the Snake River in eastern Washington, they factored in something they called "existence value"—the value of the psychic benefit people get from knowing the river is running wild.

In principle, existence value makes perfect sense. If your Aunt Agnes just can't stand the idea of people damming the Snake River, her anguish is a real cost of maintaining the dam. Of course, it's also true that if your Aunt Agnes just can't stand the idea of people reading the *New York Times*, her anguish is a real cost of allowing freedom of the press. If we're intellectually consistent, we'll cater either to both those preferences or to neither.

But why think in terms of costs and benefits in the first place? A quick—and very partial—answer is that costs and benefits are what people care about, so accounting for them is the most direct route to improving the human condition. And I like the way cost-benefit analysis treats everyone equally: a cost counts as a cost, no matter who bears it; a benefit counts as a benefit, no matter who reaps it.

My students frequently object that on the contrary, cost-benefit analysis gives the rich too much clout. If my favorite climbing tree happens to obstruct the view from Bill Gates's living room, I might be willing to pay $100 to preserve that tree while Bill is willing to pay $500,000 to destroy it. Chopping down the tree imposes a $100 cost on me while conferring a $500,000 benefit on Bill, so—at least if we are true cost-benefit believers—the tree should go. The rich guy wins.

To this there are several rejoinders. First, it's worth noting that if we'd been arguing over a business asset instead of a tree, Bill's wealth would be irrelevant. If an asset can add $1,000 to his profits, then that's what he's willing to pay for it, quite independent of whether he's poor or rich.

Second, in the case of the tree, it's absolutely true that Bill's wealth is a huge advantage. But there are a *lot* of contexts where wealth is a huge advantage. Take the real-estate market, for example. Bill ended up with a bigger house than mine for reasons not unrelated to our relative incomes. Maybe you think that's also a bad outcome, but if so, then your beef is not with the cost-benefit criterion; it's with the distribution of wealth. You can believe wealth is distributed unfairly and still believe in cost-benefit analysis, just as you can believe wealth is distributed unfairly and still believe that houses should be sold to the highest bidder.

On the other hand—and I warn you right now that I have an unlimited supply of other hands—there is (at least) one important difference between getting the bigger house and being allowed to dispose of the tree: Bill *paid* for his house, which means he'll have a little less wealth and a little less clout in future transactions. In the case of the tree, he got his victory for free, which somehow seems more objectionable. That's a legitimate distinction. But again, it's a concern that can be addressed without abandoning the cost-benefit philosophy: if Bill really values his view at $500,000, then make him pay me $300,000 for the privilege of cutting down the tree. That way, he and I can *both* be happier. And in fact, if I own the tree, that's exactly what happens.

If you want a *real* cost-benefit conundrum, try this one, courtesy of Judge Richard Posner of the Seventh Circuit Court of Appeals. Suppose I'm willing to pay $100,000 to wrap you in barbed wire and zap you with cattle prods, and you'd accept no less than $50,000 to let me. That's a $100,000 benefit to me and a $50,000 cost to you, so all good cost-benefit analysts agree that I should be allowed to wrap you in barbed wire and zap you with cattle prods. And in fact, that's exactly what will happen, as long as you and I can sit down and negotiate a payment of (say) $75,000. Everyone—you and I and the cost-benefit analyst—walks away happy.

But let's add a diabolical twist: my pleasure depends on torturing you *nonconsensually*. Paying you off, and knowing you'll walk away happy, completely ruins my experience. Now what?

On pure cost-benefit grounds, I still get to torture you, and you don't get paid. By a strict cost-benefit criterion, rich sadists get to torture anyone they want. That's a lot more disturbing than letting Bill Gates cut down a tree, and I've never met anyone who thinks it's the right solution to this problem. I conclude that nobody—or at least nobody I've ever met—believes that cost-benefit analysis is the be-all and end-all of policy evaluation. We care also about values like dignity and freedom. Surely that's a good thing, but it does mean we've got some uncomfortable balancing to do.

Here's another uncomfortable question for the cost-benefit practitioner: who counts?

The answer is surely "everyone," but that still leaves plenty of room for dispute. Is an unborn fetus part of "everyone"? The answer surely matters if you're applying cost-benefit analysis to the abortion debate. Do costs to the fetus count or don't they? For that matter, is a cow part of "everyone"? The answer surely matters if you're debating the ethics of vegetarianism.

To apply cost-benefit analysis, you first have to decide whether the fetus counts as a full-fledged person, but once you've decided that, the cost-benefit analysis is largely superfluous. And if general cost-benefit principles tell us nothing about how to treat the unborn, they most certainly tell us nothing about how to treat the unconceived. Do we have any moral obligation to account for the interests of trillions of *potential* people, who will never have the opportunity to live unless we conceive them?

The two possible answers—"yes" and "no"—both strike me as obviously wrong. If the answer is yes, it would appear that we are morally obligated to have vast numbers of children. If the unconceived have moral status, they're like prisoners being held in a sort of limbo, unable to break through into the world of the living, and surely we are obligated to help some of them escape. (In Chapter 2, I argued that we should have more children for the benefit of those who are already living. But if you buy *this* argument, then we should have vastly *more* children for the benefit of those children themselves.) That feels all wrong to me.

But if the answer is no—if the unconceived have *no* moral status—then surely there can be no moral objection to our trashing the entire earth, to the point where there will *be* no future generations. (That's not to say that we'd necessarily *want* to trash the earth; we might have selfish reasons for preserving it. It says only that if we ever *did* want to trash the earth, it would be morally permissible.) If we prevent future generations from being conceived in the first place, and if the unconceived don't count as moral entities, then our crimes have no victims, so they're not true crimes.

So if the unconceived have rights, we get one set of disturbing conclusions, and if they don't have rights, we get a different set of disturbing conclusions. Perhaps there's a third way, and that's just to admit that we're incapable of being logically rigorous about issues involving the unconceived. Let me offer some evidence for that.

Surely you know couples like this: they already have two children, and they're undecided about whether to have a third. They waver back and forth; they lean one way and then the other; they weigh the pros and they weigh the cons. Finally they decide to go ahead. And from the instant that third child is born, the parents love it so deeply that they'd gladly sacrifice all their assets to preserve its life.

Compare that to the way people shop for appliances or furniture or compact discs. Ordinarily, the products you hesitate over are not the ones you end up treasuring most deeply. There are exceptions, of course—sometimes that CD is surprisingly good once you get it home—but the general rule is that if you weren't sure you wanted it, it's unlikely to be cherished. Why, then, are children so different?

One of my colleagues maintains that there's no real inconsistency here. He says it's wrong to think of a baby as the equivalent of a microwave oven; instead you should think of it as the equivalent of an addictive drug. People hesitate about whether to try heroin; once they've decided to try it, they become addicted and can't give it up. Likewise with babies.

But that, I think, is a very bad analogy, because heroin addicts tend to be people who believed at the outset that they could escape addiction. Perhaps that's because they're foolish, or perhaps it's because they're high-stakes gamblers, but that *is* what they were thinking. (Why else would we hear so many addicts recounting their experiences with the phrase "If only I had known . . ."?) That's not true of parents. Parents know in advance, and with near certainty, that they will be addicted to their children. They choose their addiction with eyes wide open, just like a customer choosing a microwave oven.

Moreover—and here is the key difference between parents and heroin addicts—parents know in advance, with near certainty, that they won't *want* to break their addiction. If you've already got two kids and are wavering over a third, then you've already got a pretty good idea what parenthood is like, and you already know that, unlike the addict who despises his addiction, you're going to *treasure* your attachment to your children. When you know you're going to love something that much after you've got it, how can you hesitate about getting it in the first place?

But as the parent of an only child, I can verify that people do behave that way. I know that my unconceived children would be my most valuable "possessions" if I brought them to fruition, yet

I've chosen to leave them unconceived. Is it possible there's just no logic here?

If this whole discussion strikes you as the sort of idle Sunday dorm-room chitchat that kept you from studying for your chemistry final but never amounted to anything of practical importance, I beg to differ. Whenever we talk about critical real-world policy issues like, say, reforming the Social Security system, we are implicitly talking about our obligations to future generations who are not yet conceived. It is impossible to discuss those obligations sensibly without figuring out what they are.

Of course, much of the Social Security debate is notoriously nonsensible (or nonsensical) to begin with; rhetoric on all sides is littered with meaningless references to lockboxes, trust funds, and other accounting tricks that have absolutely nothing to do with the underlying economics.

Here's the underlying economics. In the year 2050, there will be some young people and some old people. Depending on how hard those people work, there will also be some quantity of goods and services to distribute. The people of 2050 will essentially face four questions: How hard should young people work? How hard should old people work? What fraction of the resulting goods and services should young people consume? And what fraction should old people consume?

The answers to those questions will be fought out in the legislatures of 2050, largely without regard to any laws we pass today. So if we want to help those future citizens, our accounting rules and other financial shenanigans are quite irrelevant. All we can do—insofar as we want to help out—is consume less, so there's more left over for the future. We'll leave them more and better factories, they'll produce more and better goods, and they'll distribute those goods in ways we can't constrain.

Therefore there are only two meaningful questions about Social Security. First, do we want to consume less so our grandchildren can consume more? And second, if that's what we want to do, how can we get ourselves to do it?

One answer to the second question is that we can encourage saving through favorable tax treatment. Or we can encourage saving by phasing out Social Security, which would probably encourage at least some people to save more. The cost of those reforms is that we'd have to tighten our own belts. Saving more means consuming less. Phasing out Social Security payments means facing a lot of very cranky 75-year-olds.

Whether we want to make those sacrifices depends on who we care about. If we're willing to royally screw the current generation of 70- and 80-year-olds by shutting the Social Security system down tomorrow, we can enrich all future generations from now to eternity. That's because people would immediately begin saving more, which is no more painful than paying Social Security taxes but has the advantage of yielding more investment, hence more factories and more productive capacity, constantly replenished through ongoing saving. Bottom line: we devastate several million old people today and enrich a potentially unlimited number in the future.

On strict cost-benefit grounds, that's a good deal—*if* we count all those future generations as heavily as we count those who are with us today. (Yes, I realize it's completely unfair to the currently old, which is why I used the phrase "royally screw." The point remains that we're doing even more good than harm.) One excellent argument says that people are people whenever they're born, so of *course* we should count them all equally. An opposing excellent argument says that (a) we have no moral obligation to reproduce in the first place and (b) if we're not even required to give these people *life*, then surely we're not required to give them *wealth*.

Two excellent arguments, diametrically opposed in their conclusions. Excuse me while I squirm.

Reforming (or abolishing) Social Security should appeal to people who care a lot about future generations—in other words, the sort of people who support environmental conservation. Both conservation and Social Security reform take from the currently living to give to the not-yet-born. So, by and large, I'd expect supporters of one to be well-disposed toward the other.

If you're trying to decide where you stand on those issues, you might keep in mind that the not-yet-born are likely to be a whole lot richer than you and me—I calculated in Chapter 2 that in just 400 years, our descendants are likely to have incomes in excess of $1 million a day. So if you're against Social Security or in favor of conservation, you're really out to transfer a lot of income from the relatively poor—namely you and me—to the relatively rich— namely our fabulously wealthy grandchildren. It would be intellectually jarring to hold that position while supporting a large welfare state that's designed to transfer income from the rich to the poor.

So to a first approximation, I expect some people (those who care more about the poor, and hence more about the currently living) to advocate for welfare programs, ongoing Social Security, and less conservation, while other people (those who care more about the rich, and hence more about future generations) to advocate for less welfare, Social Security cuts, and more conservation.

Of course there's far more to each of these issues, and I'm sure there are perfectly coherent intellectual bases for any package of policies you can imagine. But some packages, more than others, have at least a whiff of inconsistency about them. Inconsistency also makes me squirm.

Unsure as I am of how to treat the unborn, the not-yet-born, and the never-to-be-conceived, I turn my attention to the long-departed. Should we care about the preferences of the dead?

Well, of course not, because the dead have no preferences; that's part of being dead. But what about the preferences they *used* to have? Preferences like "Don't harvest my organs" or "Don't keep me on a ventilator after I'm brain dead" or "Scatter my ashes from the visitor's gallery at the New York Stock Exchange"?

Sometimes we honor the preferences of the dead because we think the dead were unusually wise, or because "letting the dead decide" is a good rule for settling disputes without bloodshed; those are the reasons we look to the U.S. Constitution for guidance, but they don't seem particularly relevant here. The other reason to honor dead people's preferences—to enforce their wills, for example—is to alter their behavior *before* they die. If you promise me that my estate will go to my daughter instead of some random stranger, I'll work more and consume less—which means everyone else can afford to work less and consume more. (After all, everything I produce and don't consume is available for someone else, and available *immediately,* not just after I die.) That's a good reason to promise you'll enforce my will, and it's also a good reason to *keep* that promise, so other people will believe such promises in the future.

On the other hand, I see far less reason why you should let me dictate the disposal of my remains. I might have strong preferences about the matter, but once I'm gone, those preferences are quite irrelevant, and while I'm alive, your promise to enforce those preferences is unlikely to change my behavior in any socially useful way.

Thomas Jefferson (one of those dead wise men to whom we sometimes turn for advice) admonished us that the earth belongs to the living, by which he meant that we can safely ignore the preferences of the dead. Once they stop living, it's frivolous to care what they prefer.

But what about the preferences of the survivors? Take a case in point: Terri Schiavo, a woman attached to a ventilator and believed to be in a permanent state of unconsciousness tantamount to death, became a national cause célèbre when her husband and her parents could not agree on whether to unplug her.*

The Schiavo battle was over the control of a resource, namely Ms. Schiavo's body, and was therefore well within the purview of economic analysis. Ms. Schiavo's husband, Michael, wanted to dispose of the body; her parents wanted to feed it. The question then arises: once someone has decided to dispose of a resource, why would we want to stop someone else from retrieving it? If I throw out a toaster, and you want to retrieve it from my trash, there's a net economic gain. If Michael Schiavo essentially throws out his wife's body and her parents want to retrieve it, it seems pointless to prevent them.

Except for the fact that Michael Schiavo *wanted* to prevent

---

* There was and is considerable controversy about Ms. Schiavo's actual condition. I have absolutely no expertise that would allow me to have an interesting opinion about that controversy. The analysis in this chapter takes it as given, for the sake of argument, that Ms. Schiavo was unrecoverable.

them, and the rules of the cost-benefit game require us to presume that all human wants should be respected. Except I'm not so sure about that.

I've already entertained an exception for censorship, and I think that same exception applies here. A preference to prevent someone else from doing something he wants to do, just for the sake of stopping him, is not, I suspect, a preference we want to cater to. That's a very dangerous position, because it raises all sorts of questions about where to draw the line, and I have no idea how to answer most of those questions. But the alternative, it seems to me, is to endorse the tyranny of the bluenoses.

Now, Michael Schiavo, it seems to me, was in something very like the bluenose position here. If he'd had a use for his wife's body—if he'd wanted to cook it up for dinner, let's say—then I'd have more sympathy for him. (On the other hand, I don't think we should make a habit of letting people cook their spouses for dinner, because it creates very bad incentives with regard to keeping your spouse safe and healthy.) But in fact, he never wanted to do anything at all with the body, except perhaps to bury it, in accord with what he perceived to be the wishes of an essentially dead woman whose wishes had long since ceased to count. His only desire was to stop someone else from feeding the body, and I see very little difference between that and wanting to stop someone else from reading *Lady Chatterley's Lover*.

Well, one difference is that I enthusiastically understand why people read D. H. Lawrence, and I have less understanding of why people want to keep feeding relatives who are essentially dead. And insofar as they want *others* to keep feeding her—through Medicare, for example—I think we can safely ignore their preferences. But provided they are willing to bear those costs, I infer that this is something they want very much and there's not much reason to stop them.

In fact, Michael Schiavo signaled an equally strong desire to bury her (by turning down an offer of $1 million and by some reports $10 million), but I see an essential difference between the two desires. One—the desire to feed—is like the desire to read *Lady Chatterley,* or, more precisely, the desire to read some other work in which I personally see no literary merit. The other—the desire to prevent others from feeding—is like the desire to censor, and I recoil from censorship even when a strict cost-benefit analysis recommends it.

The philosophical and economic arguments for cost-benefit-based policy-making fill many textbooks, and this is not the place to summarize them. Suffice it to say that most people who have studied those arguments find them broadly convincing, though nobody (to my knowledge) finds them universally compelling. The question is where to draw the line.

I am inclined to draw the line somewhere north of a preference for controlling other people's behavior. If porn on the Internet, oil drilling in Alaska, or scavengers in your trash bin offend you, then I cheerfully acknowledge that offense as a genuine cost, but I choose not to count it in my policy analysis.

I make that choice with some trepidation, because I have no clear principled reason for drawing the line where I do. If you object to oil drilling in a place you plan to visit, I'm inclined to count that; if you object to oil drilling in a place you visit only in your daydreams, I'm inclined not to. I think I have some pretty good reasons for those inclinations, but I wish I had better ones.

I feel the same trepidation when I'm forced to think about how to account for future generations. And I feel it most acutely in the face of market failures—as in Philadelphia—that can clearly be alleviated by government action, but only by whittling away a bit of freedom.

If we tax every spillover cost and subsidize every spillover benefit, then in principle the communal stream should run clearer. But excessive government is also a pollutant, and we probably want to keep that in mind, too.

APPENDIX

Here are some sources, suggestions for further reading, and additional arguments.

Preface: Unconventional Wisdom I don't know who first said "Common sense is what tells you the earth is flat," but you can find it on a button at my favorite repository of wit and wisdom, the catalogue at http://www.nancybuttons.com.

One more example might be helpful:

When General Motors builds a new factory, the world gets more cars (which is good) but at a cost—the cars are built by workers who might otherwise be milking cows or laying cable or making sandwiches, so somebody somewhere has to drink less milk or wait an extra week for a cable hookup or wake up fifteen minutes earlier to pack his own lunch. The factory occupies land that might otherwise house a bakery or an artist's studio, so the world has to get by with less bread or fewer paintings.

Fortunately, GM feels all those costs and all the benefits. They pay for land and the workers at prices that reflect their value in alternative uses; they sell cars at prices that reflect their value to consumers. If the benefits exceed the costs, they build the factory; if not, not. Just as things ought to be.

But that calculation goes out the window if the factory is destined, say, to pollute a communal stream (or to produce cars that pollute the atmosphere). Pollution is a real social cost (which is just a fancy way of saying it hurts someone), but GM might not account for it. In that case, GM builds too many factories—just as check-splitters order too many desserts.

1. More Sex Is Safer Sex Michael Kremer's AIDS research appeared in the *Quarterly Journal of Economics* under the title "Integrating Behavioral Choice into Epidemiological Models of the AIDS Epidemic."

2. Be Fruitful and Multiply Michael Kremer's research on population growth appeared in the *Quarterly Journal of Economics* under the title "Population Growth and Technological Change: One Million BC to 1990." For a gripping account of how millennia of economic stagnation yielded to the Industrial Revolution, see "The Industrial Revolution: Past and Future" by Nobel laureate Robert E. Lucas, Jr., in the *Region* (published by the Federal Reserve Bank of Minneapolis). For the effects of economic growth on the life of the average housewife, see "Engines of Liberation" by Jeremy Greenwood, Ananth Seshadri, and Mehmet Yörükoğlu in the *Review of Economic Studies*. The effects of parental leave in Austria were established by Professors Rafael Lalive and Josef Zweimüller of the University of Zurich; their paper, titled "Does Parental Leave Affect Fertility and

Return-to-Work? Evidence from a 'True Natural Experiment'"
has not yet (as of this writing) been published.

4. Who's the Fairest of Them All? The effects of beauty
on wages were established by Professors Daniel Hamermesh
(University of Texas) and Jeff Biddle (Michigan State), writing in
the *American Economic Review*. The effects of obesity on wages
were established by Professor John Cawley (Cornell), writing in
the *Journal of Human Resources*. The clever economists at the
University of Pennsylvania who figured out *why* height breeds
success were Nicola Persico, Andrew Postlewaite, and Dan Silverman; Silverman is now at the University of Michigan. The tall
and intelligent Princeton economists who attributed the
height/wage correlation to differences in intelligence are Anne
Case and Christine Paxson. Their paper on "Stature and Status:
Height, Ability and Labor Market Outcomes" is not yet published (as of this writing). The CMP (Cole, Mailath, Postlewaite)
research appeared in the *Journal of Political Economy* under the
title "Social Norms, Savings Behavior and Growth."

5. Children at Work The withdrawal of third-world children from the labor market as incomes rise is established by
Cornell Professor Kaushik Basu and then World Bank researcher Zafiris Tzannatos in a thoughtful and important paper
called "The Global Child Labor Problem: What Do We Know
and What Can We Do?" published in the *World Bank Economic
Review*.

6. and **7. How to Fix Politics** and **How to Fix the Justice System** Many of the ideas in these chapters were born and
nurtured over the lunch table. Many colleagues participated in

those discussions, but the best and most outrageous ideas almost always originated with Mark Bils.

7. How to Fix the Justice System For biographical facts about Reverend Bayes and life in Tunbridge Wells I am indebted to "The Reverend Thomas Bayes, FRS: A Biography to Celebrate the Tercentenary of His Birth," by D. R. Bellhouse, writing in *Statistical Science*. Isaac Ehrlich and Zhiqiang Liu's most recent work on the death penalty appeared in a paper called "Sensitivity Analyses of the Deterrence Hypothesis: Let's Keep the Econ in Econometrics," published in the *Journal of Law and Economics*. See also the many papers in "The Economics of Crime," a three-volume compendium of readings edited by Ehrlich and Liu and published by Edward Elgar in 2006.

In this chapter, I've concentrated on improving the justice system we've got. David Friedman, a professor of law at the University of Santa Clara, advocates a far more radical reform: scrap the system entirely, in favor of a privatized legal system with competing governments offering a variety of legal codes. You'd choose the code you want to live by, and sign up with the government that offers it. According to Friedman, such systems have worked well historically, most strikingly for several centuries in medieval Iceland. In a Friedmanesque world, where you swim in the legal stream of your choice, changes in a particular legal code would affect only voluntary subscribers, minimizing spillover effects.

8. How to Fix Everything Else Michael Kremer's paper on patents appeared in the *Quarterly Journal of Economics* under the title "Patent Buy-Outs: A Mechanism for Encouraging Innovation." Levitt and Ayres's paper on the LoJack appeared in the *Quarterly Journal of Economics* under the title "Measuring

Positive Externalities from Unobservable Victim Precaution: An Empirical Analysis of LoJack." John Lott and David Mustard published their research on handgun control in the *Journal of Legal Studies* (1997). See also Lott's book *More Guns, Less Crime*. The $15,000 estimate for the market price of a kidney is from recent work of Gary Becker and Julio Jorge Elias (the University of Chicago). The idea to shorten waiting lines is based on a paper by Professor Refael Hassin (Tel Aviv University) published in *Econometrica* and titled "On the Optimality of First Come Last Served Queues." Professor Barry Nalebuff (Yale) first applied Professor Hassin's idea to the problem of water-fountain lines in his "Puzzles" column in the *Journal of Economic Perspectives*. Sometime later, having heard about Professor Nalebuff's puzzle over a lunch table and not knowing its source, I published a *Slate* column on the same topic.

Part III. Everyday Economics The pencil study by DiNardo and Pischke appeared in the *Quarterly Journal of Economics;* its title was "The Returns to Computer Use Revisited: Have Pencils Changed the Wage Structure Too?" A more recent paper by Professor Kevin Lang of Boston University, "Of Pencils and Computers," offers evidence that computers really do raise productivity.

9. Go Figure Haveman and Wolfe's findings on the effects of residential moves are reported in their book *Succeeding Generations: On the Effects of Investments in Children.*

10. Oh No! It's a Girl! Professor Dahl is now at the University of California, San Diego, and Professor Moretti is at Berkeley; their paper on "The Demand for Sons" is not yet published.

11. The High Price of Motherhood Amalia Miller's paper is called "The Effects of Motherhood Timing on Career Path"; it is not yet published.

12. Giving Your All The main idea for this chapter came from a conversation with Mark Bils, who had to explain it to me three times before I got it. Here's the math from the back of the envelope; if you don't remember your calculus, you'll want to skip this.

Suppose there are three charities (the same argument would work with any number other than three). Suppose that those charities currently have endowments of x, y, and z, and that you plan to make contributions of $\triangle x$, $\triangle y$, and $\triangle z$. A truly charitable person will care only about each charity's final endowment, and so will seek to maximize some function:

$$F(x + \triangle x, y + \triangle y, z + \triangle z)$$

(The function F is quite arbitrary. This argument assumes that you care about the charities, but makes no assumption about how or why you care.)

If your contributions are small relative to the initial endowments, this quantity is well approximated by

$$F(x, y, z) + (\partial F/\partial x)\triangle x + (\partial F/\partial y)\triangle y + (\partial F/\partial z)\triangle z$$

which is maximized by giving everything to the charity that corresponds to the largest of the partial derivatives.

The linear approximation fails if your contributions are large relative to the initial endowments, or if you have sufficient delusions of grandeur to *believe* that your contributions are large relative to the initial endowments.

Note that if you have any uncertainty about what the various charities will do with their endowments, the costs of that uncertainty can be built into the definition of the function F. Thus such uncertainty in no way undermines the main argument.

On the other hand, if you care not about what the charitable organizations receive but about what you give to them (as would be the case, for example, if you give in order to enjoy being thanked), then you will want to maximize some function

$F(\triangle x, \triangle y, \triangle z)$

In this case, it's unlikely that the solution would be to give everything to one charity.

13. The Central Banker of the Soul The paper by Professors Per Krusell (now of Princeton) and Anthony Smith (of Yale) appeared in *Econometrica* and is called "Consumption-Savings Decisions with Quasi-Geometric Discounting." The work of Professor Laibson (Harvard) includes his paper "Golden Eggs and Hyperbolic Discounting," published in the *Quarterly Journal of Economics*. I was first led to think of the Universe as a purely mathematical object by a side comment in *The Physics of Immortality*, a book by the prominent physicist Frank Tipler. For a far more thorough investigation, see "Is the 'Theory of Everything' Merely the Ultimate Ensemble Theory?" written by MIT physicist Max Tegmark and published in the *Annals of Physics*

14. How to Read the News. The analysis of racial profiling is based on work by John Knowles, Nicola Persico, and Petra Todd, all of the University of Pennysylvania; it was published recently in the *Journal of Political Economy*. Their argument is a bit subtler than I've indicated in the text. I've argued that if the police are not racially biased, then blacks and whites who are stopped and searched should be equally likely to be carrying drugs. This is no longer clearly true if other observable characteristics correlae with both race and drug carrying. For example, if it were known that all whites driving Volkswagens carry drugs, then all whites driving Volkswagens would be stopped and searched, and the average conviction rates would be higher for whites, even though the police exhibit no anti-white bias. Knowles, Persico, and Todd have a clever argument (slightly too technical for this book) that dismisses this possiblity; roughly, their argument says that if all whites driving Volkswagens carried drugs, then all whites driving Volkswagens would be stopped, so no whites driving Volkswagens would carry drugs.

15. Matters of Life and Death Professor Kip Viscusi's work on the value of life has appeared in a long series of papers, of which a good representative is "The Value of Life: Estimates with Risks by Occupation and Industry," appearing in *Economic Inquiry*. The cell-phone study by Hahn, Tetlock, and Burnett appeared in *Regulation* under the title "Should You Be Allowed to Use Your Cellular Phone While Driving?"

Baylor Regional Medical Center's detailed response about the Tirhas Habtegiris case can be found at http://www.baylor health.com/articles/habtegiris/response.htm.

INDEX

ABOUT THE AUTHOR

Steven E. Landsburg is a Professor of Economics at the University of Rochester. He is the author of *The Armchair Economist*, *Fair Play*, two textbooks on economics, and over thirty journal articles in mathematics, economics, and philosophy. He writes the popular "Everyday Economics" column in *Slate* magazine and has written for *Forbes*, the *Wall Street Journal*, and other publications.